❧A to Z Virtuous Downloads❧

An energetic method for making positive changes in your life

Robin Coventry

Enjoy Life

www.COATIplusU.com

When each and every person on this planet can see each and every person on this planet— including themselves— as a person of value, all valuable, all worthy, all precious, all unique, all equal with differences, knowing that it is OK to be different, we will see magnificent changes in the way all process of life work for humanity.

Robin Coventry

ISBN: 9781679515194

*Dedicated to spiritual teachers, students
and those helping all species on the path of life.*

I Honor You

*Special Thanks to my mother, Frances Haley, for allowing space
for me to evolve.*

To my family, with hope, I look to the day when you understand.

You are a Gem of Humanity.

Believe in YOU.

Robin Coventry

CONTENTS

Dissolve the illusions you have created
about life to uncover the beauty you
hold within.

Robin Coventry

❧ Introduction ❦

The need for self-awareness has never been more important.
Not from an egoic sense, but a deeper spiritual sense of self-
realization. Who we are becomes the energy that touches all
around our physical body. It's the thought we send across the
miles. The imprint we make in our lifetime with the ripple
affect that moves forward through genetic time. In this
incarnation of life each of us has a huge affect on our
children, families, friends, business associates and even people
you do not know. Our body's energy contributes to the
functioning of the planet and all we see. There is an
interaction or exchange of energy where ever we go and what
ever we do. Realize that you are an important part of All
That Is. You are valuable and worthy beyond measure.

As we reflect on our life and understand our idiosyncrasies we
shine a light on our talents and skills as well as those areas in
need of modification, that cause us to malfunction in our
relationships and towards ourselves. Our body's energy can
be heavy meaning a lower frequency of vibration or lightened
so we feel the unburdened difference of realignment with the
Divine Energy of the Universe. This affects not only you, but
all.

The underpinning of life is that each of us contributes to life. Each of us can make a difference in a positive or negative way in the journey of all. Our abilities are far greater than any of us have been lead to believe. There is no reason for anyone to suffer on this planet or be stagnant in their thinking. No matter who you are or where you live—it could be anywhere— you are a valuable member of the human race contributing energetically to the grid on and surrounding the earth which affects all live forms.

A to Z Virtuous Downloads is for those that know how to use downloads, those waking up to them and those who want to know more. It was created with love and compassion for the reader, the speaker and the listener. It's filled with virtues we already have, can improve on or cultivate in this lifetime. Most of the virtues you will relate too, others you may not think you will ever need. It is suggested you download them anyway, as energy is energy in this life and the next and the next. It is also energy backward into the past and our entire genetic line. Words are powerful; they are our thoughts and beliefs and the beginning of all manifestation. As you accept the virtuous downloads, variations of the words or additional phrases may come to mind, incorporate them too.

This book is a tool to use in your own spiritual progression. It does not guarantee to magically make your life perfect or rid you of disease. Vibrational imbalances are caused by things we do, likewise cleaned up by things we do. This book does not train you in any healing technique and is not a substitute for training with a professional. What it does is tell you how to use energy to give yourself and people you know downloads. If you can define it as a positive aspect of living, it can be downloaded into your energetic field.

❧ What Are Downloads? ❧

Downloads in the conventional sense are information, or files copied from the Internet, disc or from one computer system to another. Because all things are energy like the files from one computer to the next or from the Internet to your computer or cell phone, so too are your memories, thoughts and beliefs.

For purposes of this explanation, picture the brain as one of the world's most advanced computers with the ability to add or remove apps that control our very existence and how we respond to life. Our own beliefs, we could call them personal apps, cause us to react to situations in specific ways. Encoded within each personal app is energetically stored information, which can be positive or negative.

Our positive evolution requires the removal of harmful, outdated apps or beliefs that no longer serve us efficiently. Ridding ourselves of them poses a real growth challenge if we genuinely accepted or became too comfortable with a negative belief that became part of our body's physical operating system.

An example of this is when something triggers you. Your whole body may have a physical reaction. Your belly may feel uneasy, your mind races, anger may rise along with your blood pressure as breathing increases you may even sweat. The funny thing is you may not be aware it is happening before your body throws you into stress mode. Notice how subconscious beliefs of your operating system affect you. Learning to observe the unconscious reactions of your body in all situations will reveal what you need to work on.

All humans face the issue of upgrading together. By removing our outdated software programs and replacing them with new positive apps that serve us in the best of ways, we enhance our lives. I cannot emphasize the exchange of old beliefs for new ones enough. If we don't we condemn ourselves to reliving negative patterns over and over.

Understanding All That Is Energy, whether you can see it or not is an essential step in the evolutionary process. None of us are alone, but we must stand alone to modify our particular energetic field. You are one light among billions, how bright do you shine? As you clear negative debris from your energetic field your inner light shines brighter. This is also an external phenomenon. You actually glow in the dark as you rid yourself of your negative baggage. You become a lighter person.

Across the earth, there are many who can help or guide you on your spiritual path of refinement. There are pioneers trained in releasing your negative belief patterns, fears, negative emotions, resentments, regrets, grief, sorrows, hatred, lack of self love and so much more. They are as different as night and day just as you are. But they understand how to work with Source Energy to help you evolve quicker. They are here to help, as witnesses to the Great and Powerful works done by our Creator. What or who resonates with one, may not with another. That is ok. The main idea is to find what or who resonates with you. When you do, you can create a new life at any age that is fulfilling. The archaic belief "You can't teach an old dog new tricks" is a falsehood. If you are ready, help is available.

What are downloads? This word is appearing more and more in mainstream spiritual vocabulary. They could be called affirmations PLUS. Downloads are considered affirmations, beliefs and feelings intended to positively alter a person's energetic field. Active information with intention in the form of a download can make a difference by instilling positive energy of the Word into a person's heart, mind and body's energetic field. Downloads along with belief work is powerfully transforming.

Our physical body and morphogenetic field are energy. We add all kinds of thoughts, memories and beliefs into that field over the course of a life. If negative energy goes it, it can also come out. We, can also insert positives into our own field to enhance our lives via a connection to Source and positive intent.

❧Programming Life❧

Science discovered the best way to accept and retain downloads is when a person is in the theta brainwave frequency. Dr. Patrick Gannon PhD in *The Neuroscience of Peak Performance and Flow* found, "Flow state is located at the crossover point between alpha and theta brain waves. As brain activity slows from the relaxing alpha wave into the hypnagogic theta wave, the neural network becomes highly attuned." Hypnotherapy works in the alpha/theta brain wave frequencies. These frequencies promote learning and remembrance.

Through EEG research science found that children from age two to roughly age seven live in the theta programmable state of mind. Dr. Bruce Lipton, author of *Biology of Belief* says "A child's perception of the world are directly downloaded into the subconscious during this time without discrimination and without filters of the analytical self-conscious mind which doesn't fully exist. Consequently, our fundamental perceptions about life and our role in it are learned without our having the capacity to choose or reject those beliefs. We are simply programmed."

While in the theta state children walk around in a hypnogogic trance; a state where significant beliefs of life are made concrete or fixed into the subconscious energetic field. Early conditioning or programming builds the foundation for a child's life negatively or positively. If children experience self-sabotage, unworthiness, lack of love, anger, rejection, resentment or misperceptions, that is what becomes a child's ingrained truth of life unless they do something to change the negative patterns and beliefs that haunt them as an adult. If denied love, children may grow into an adult with beliefs that cause them to respond to life negatively. Each of us is worthy of love whether we know it or not, which is why loving care should be a part of all child rearing.

In the channeled book series by Dr. Frank Alper, he wrote in book one of *Exploring Atlantis* that In Atlantean times, adults gave birth to children to bring a newly incarnated being into the world. The embodied soul came to earth with a life mission. A set of parents had their children for the first year but did not go on to raise their children. After a year, children were raised in a community of women called mothers. In their society, no one owned children like they do today. CITE: Alper, Frank Dr. Exploring Atlantis book one, Quantum Productions 1981

The Atlantean way allowed children to be protected and raised without the afflictions that society could place upon them. Souls incarnating to Atlantis had a chance to develop their talents and life purpose a lot sooner. This type of child rearing created a stable life foundation for the developing adult. It allowed information of the purest sort to be learned or accepted into a child's operating system. Knowledge, as we know, is power; for the sake of humanity, using it harmoniously for the higher good shows true wisdom.

We are responsible for our self, that includes what we do and how we live or BE-Have (behave). If you have a family, you may be saying I am responsible for more than myself. Yes, you have a greater responsibility to build a strong foundation for your child, so they grow up as well-adjusted, loving adults.

But you are not the keeper of their spirits. They are. They came here just like you to gain new insights and learn. It is the children that will live to unite humanity. Before we reach new levels of understanding, we must evolve to higher levels of consciousness by attaining knowledge and using it for the highest benefit. Are you scratching your head and wondering, how can I develop if I do not have experience? Or maybe you are thinking where do I acquire this knowledge?

Each of us has a purpose or assignment in life, a reason for existing that is a part of our spiritual evolution. I use the word human because we are all HU Mans or humankind (as called) as a species. HU is an ancient term for God Being that is free from gender. The word man represents a patriarchal identifier for people on earth. Hence we are god man or men and I will add women (womb man—man with a womb).

All life forms find themselves mutually connected to the Highest form of energy; the Creator Force or as some prefer, God. I could list the numerous names for Source Energy but choose to allow you to broaden your perceptions of Allah. Because that Energy is in each of us, we can be called human. We are all extensions of the Ultimate Energy of the Universe, which is a reason to be judgment-free, for how can we judge our Mother-Father- God? How can you look at someone and only see faults? You are looking at Yahweh, Jehovah and the Ancient of Days when you gaze at people. Can you see it? Can you accept it? It is part of your evolutionary process. To free your mind and open your heart to the Divine Love that flows freely to all inhabitants of earth.

By focusing on understanding, thinking and speaking about the positive attributes of people we become self-aware and realize we are all connect as a life force on earth. We are connected to the greatest operating system that is ever expanding, ever growing, ever seeking to spread love to all life forms. We humans get caught in nets of negativity cast out to keep us in the dark as to our true spirituality. It is time for the light to shine and the knowledge we have all forgotten to be remembered. We are all worthy, capable beings that can accomplish great actions or things. It is time to draw on that energy to resolve all human conflicts and bring humanity to a place in time where we honor and respect the Divine in all.

Collectively, our purpose is to learn to allow our spirit to reach new levels of a higher thought or being, which involves clearing the debris from our specific energetic field. When we learn to clear, we become lighter as the photons in our bodies glow brighter, and then we shine, making us more of a light being on the path to enlightenment. As we study to break away from the current system that has kept us in the dark, we become lightened women or men. Let's break down the word Enlightenment. In Lightened (wo)Men(t), or In Light Human. I add the (wo) to be inclusive. Are you living and walking in the Light? Inlighthuman is not found in dictionaries, but this word carries what is happening to each of us if we choose to lighten our load. Enlightenment.

Free will is used to devolve or evolve. It is your personal choice, not that of anyone else on the path you chose. When we open ourselves up to Creator, the very energy that keeps our heart beating, we expand our consciousness and grow. Knowledge and wisdom are available to help you on your way if you decide to open the door of your heart and mind. Teachers come when you are ready in the form of a person, an article, workshop, book, conference, or an idea that downloads to you. This is all part of the symphony of life ever flowing.

The following experience is a different kind of download

> I was standing in my room one afternoon with my eyes open, not thinking about anything in particular when I felt a subtle surge of energy. In my minds eye I could see flashes of dozens of geometric shapes coming into me. The designs were intricately complex, colorful and like nothing I had ever seen. Along with the sacred geometry, I saw a movie of a long curved line of people from all cultures both men, women and children moving forward in time. Their physical appearance and attire were all different and unique. A deep knowing filled me; I knew they were me in past incarnations. You may be wondering about the many geometric shapes. I believe they were an upgrade or energetic insertion of sacred geometry into my energetic field unlocking new abilities and revealing new thought.

Where did the Energy come from? From All That Is, for the Energy was as loving and awe-inspiring as anything I have ever experienced. My deep love for Source Energy, has never been stronger. Divine Love creates no boundaries, no borders amongst humankind. It is the ultimate unifier. The purest essence of a love energy stronger more comforting than human words in any language can express. Each and every person on this planet, no matter their life path, is worthy of the embrace of Divine Love that fills our senses.

❧ Frequencies ❧

Today, a significant need exists for therapeutic treatments that undo the baggage created by life experiences, which are necessary for humanity to evolve. Everything around us is frequency and has a specific vibrational level. From the previous paragraph, there is a shift to a lower frequency to discuss and shine light on what has happened. Each of us has a vibrational energy level or energy signature that is unique to us. How can this be said? No one on earth has had the exact life experiences as you. Yes, you may know people with similar shared events that caused emotional registers in their energetic field or one that were precisely the same. However, we never have the exact compositional life experience. I can say this for we all see life from a different perspective because of every single occurrence in our lives and our familial genetics.

Our beliefs are structured by genetics and life experience that raises or lowers the body's energetic frequency. Every body's conglomerate of mixed energy over time creates a unique energetic signature or song that identifies them at any given moment. This frequency can be heard if you sit in a quiet place. You can hear your own tone in your ears as a vibration. It is good to tune into your own tone and meditate as you listen. Your energy is All That Is Energy that can be heavy or light; the lighter the being the higher the vibration.

Some of humanity has become comfortable accepting lower frequencies and therefore create disease in their bodies, and a multitude of suffering. Each charge of emotion is energy stored in the collection of organs, systems and energetic field which is the container or home of our energetic spirit that powers the human body or meat suit. If we overload our bodies with negatively charged emotions, disease that is in alignment with the frequency of the negatively charged emotion begins to grow. You may know someone whose cancer grew or disease manifested after a tragic event, loss, or even extreme grief. There body was in overload and disease came upon them.

We assume that life "Is what it is," and will continue as it is. There is some truth in this but upon evaluation it is a flawed premise. This brings to mind a phrase I once heard and refer back to again and again.

"We don't know what we don't know, until we know it."

This phrase allows us to expand into creating new realities. Each of us has a point of reality that marks our life; a system that protects us from mental overload. We can as in the case of this book choose to expand our belief system with accepting reassurance that there is more to life than what is perceive in our own reality.

I am not referring to travel luggage. I am referring to the emotional memories people carry day in and day out. Where does baggage come from? It could go all the way back to childhood. It comes from life's negative experiences. You may have heard someone say "He's got a lot of baggage." Now, the guy could be a world traveller, but we are referring to life's negative debris that builds up for all to feel and see. Each person's negative experiences are unlike anyone else's because they all come from your own evolved perspective.

So, Is your suitcase full, partially full or empty? What are you carrying through life? How heavy is your load? Answers to these questions are your own and belong to no one else. All you have known, witnessed, or lived in life has left an imprinted frequency density, which adds to your physical body's total vibration. Your imprinting can be positive or negative; rest assured that moments of our lives wield great strength over the subconscious mind and how we respond to living.

Your life's occurrences (memories) are not stored on sheets of paper in a filing cabinet for you to recall them as needed; unless you kept a diary. They are stored as memories, which are invisible frequencies held in the energetic field both in and around the body.

To change a vibrational frequency, a person has to be aware of what adds to it positively or negatively. We have to understand that all stored energies from events in life become part of our programming or belief system, as mentioned earlier. Beliefs can be simple or quite complicated.

Example One

If your parents programmed you to grow up to be in the same profession as a father or mother and you decided not to do as you were told, you might feel guilty or have an underlying belief that you failed or let your parents down because you did not follow your family tradition. Your body retains that energy until you learn to release it.

Example Two

If an alcoholic raised you, the emotions and feelings associated with that type of life mutated your energetic field. That type of energy is familiar to your cellular receptors. Your unconscious body will unknowingly be drawn to alcoholics. Perhaps a pattern developed over time of you getting involved in a relationship with one alcoholic after another. Why? Because your cellular receptors were programmed to seek out those that fit the energetic pattern that is most familiar or programmed by your life.

Example Three

You grew up with a sense of security as your loving parents nurtured you and allowed you to develop and grow in a healthy environment. You were fed healthy organic foods that nourished your body and were kept from harmful chemicals in preservatives, to much sugar or vaccinations that degrade the body. You learned it was safe to trust and believe in people of all cultures. Your energetic field and belief systems are free from a lot of negative debris. This allows you to tap easily into the powerful abilities each human has from birth.

Example Four
If you as a child were taught to play with toy soldiers or electronic war games, that killed animals or people that became part of your programming. How about being raised to play with dolls or care for them? You were programmed to become a nurturer. When children are turned over to public school systems, they are programmed to believe a specific way on many topics, whether they are true or not.

Do you as an adult fill your ears with songs that degrade, abuse or align with a form of sadness? Entertainment plays a role in your belief systems. Do you watch war movies or films that desensitize you to murder, unharmonious situations or a disregard for species on earth? If so, take care that you do not become a part of negative groupthink associated with some forms of entertainment. How often have you listened to a song and then could not stop thinking about it? Was it a positive loop of music or negative? Do you end up thinking about the shows you binge watch or compare them to life?

❧Programming and Genetics❧

One of the big mental programs during my era was "you only use a small portion of your brain." How could that programming possibly help humanity? It keeps a portion of our brains in a unproductive state. Why create a belief that keeps us from using our full potential? Who benefited by shutting us down? The answers to those questions are for you to ponder.

Our heart brain connection was created to help our bodies evolve. They are capable of far more than we were lead to believe. The energy that makes up our human body works in harmony until we allow dis-ease to take root. What we know as our physical body has an innate intelligence. The powerful heart-brain connection is orchestrating the physical container of our eternal spirit. Are you familiar with the phrase "Think with your mind not your heart?" This is also a form of programming. You see more of us need to think with our hearts which is the most powerful connection we have to the Creator. Hearts are wise and will never lead a person into an egoic situation like the human mind will.

 Have you ever considered the beliefs you unconsciously created because of your life experiences? Have you looked at your life's programming? As an example, did you have a happy and carefree childhood? Did loving parents nurture you? Were their parents nurturing to them? Were you encouraged to learn new things and be adventurous? Did you have stable relationships throughout your youth? Did your relatives give you positive life experiences? How about the people you knew or the ones you did not know? If you answered no to any of those questions, there is work to be done. If you answered yes, your work will be in different areas.

Negative feelings (energy) surrounding a person, event, or situation like fear, regrets, sorrow, pain, shock, trauma, anger, resentment or the ones that created a sense of unworthiness or feelings of being unloved weigh a light body down. The ultimate objective is to free yourself from negative emotions (vibrations) lightening your load. Remember, change is good when it comes to your spiritual evolution.

Each of us has something positive to add to our energetic field. Some of us require a lot of work, while others have very little. It all depends on your ancestors and life experiences.

Ancestors play a role in our evolution. The energies of your lineage are a part of you through DNA. Historical family energy followed you into this lifetime. Ancestors that fought and hated a specific race of people carried that energy in their own energetic field. You through their lineage inherited genes that make you predisposed to subconsciously feel a certain way. Your physical body through muscle testing can reveal the genetic secrets you hold, if you know what questions to ask.

If a person had an ancestor that was not nurtured as a child or found that if they became a victim or were sick all the time, they got people to care for them it felt like love. This could create a victim mentality in life.

If someone in your family lineage always tries to solve everyone else's issues, it comes from a subconscious need to validate themselves to feel worthy. They subconsciously look for approval, which could have been an attempt to please a parent that was not nurturing. Some decide to buy love by giving gifts all the time. Doing so gives momentary satisfaction but does not address the bottom belief or underlying cause of feeling unworthy.

Were you ever yelled at and told you were bad as a child? Were you rejected, shamed, spanked or beaten? How did that make you feel? Unworthy? Unloved? Much of the baggage of life comes down to emotions and associated feelings, subconscious, or unconscious beliefs of being unworthy or unloved. How was it added too? Negative vibrations of feelings and emotions can be inflicted by societal norms, school, college, jobs, accidents, parents, friends, relatives, television, a negative experience, fear, strangers, change, peers, entertainment even the food we eat. Negative energies are part of living in this current system, but that does not mean we have to retain or perpetuate such energies.

❧ Resources ❦

There are many questions to ask when we evaluate the culmination of our life up to this precise point in time. A great book to read is *Feelings Buried Alive Never Die* by Karol K. Truman. This author makes valid points about illness in the body and the dis-ease it causes. Her lists are beneficial in determining the causation of disease. Another is a book by Louise Hay, *Heal Your Body*, which discusses the emotions tied to illness in the body. Two books I use for reference are *Healer's Handbook for Practitioners* by Michael J. Lincoln Ph.D. and *The Key to Self-Liberation* by Christiane Beerlandt. All these books help you determine the psychological origins of dis-ease in the body.

How do I personally use those books? When working with clients, I can get a clear picture of what is going on with them before a session. Then allow them to tell their story, which gives me a clear picture of the root of their issue. Then I read them the pre-session information related to the named disease in their body. Most times they are shocked to see the root cause spelled out in a session then revealed by my pre-session work for them.

According to Michael J. Lincoln Ph.D. in the *Healer's Handbook* "The key factor in all this is the thought form or pattern of consciousness in the mind and soul, which affects the body... When something is awry in our consciousness, the body is the place where our consciousness problem that is precipitating the disorder, is played out."

So, what does that mean? It means when our body gets overloaded with "stuff" physical affects materialize. Something else, the subconscious mind stores your memories and beliefs and offers them up when you need or don't need them. Have you ever noticed or experienced something that triggers an emotionally charged issue from your past? Being triggered could happen from seeing someone, from a television program or hearing about a similar negative situation even a smell. Those feelings buried alive are charged with negative energy and cause your body memory to react to similar occurrences by throwing it to the surface, "Here you go, you can relate to that. Remember this?"

You may be surprised at what I say next but be grateful for your triggers for they expose something you need to release from your energetic field. They reveal parts of you that need work. It is worth your while and spiritual well being to objectively pay attention to your triggers, then work on healing the energy you hold for them.

❧ Theta Brainwave ❧

In the theta state of mind, significant changes are made to a person's belief system. We can rid ourselves of the triggers of life, sorrows, regrets, resentments and pain. Many turn to hypnotists who use the theta state to pull and download new information into their clients. Adults both practitioners or through self or group meditation have learned how to get themselves into a theta state of mind to change their belief system. These positive changes alter the very foundation of a person's life. Remember, everything is energy. All is stored as encoded energy in a body's electromagnetic field to create the person you are. You must know, this energy can change and because Energy likes change.

Getting to the theta state of mind requires concentration in a meditative state. The more you relax into the theta brainwave frequency, the easier it becomes. Like many modalities and skills the more you use it the easier it becomes.

If we can be programmed in a theta state we can also be deprogrammed. Significant change can occur as we lighten the load as the negative dissolves away. Negatively charged issues from the past whether they are genetic, are pulled or cleared from our body by a skilled practitioner. But know, you can learn to do this yourself. Then have positive downloaded information replace the negative emotionally charged feelings that can cause dis—ease in human bodies.

One quick way to do this is with Theta Healing®, a modality created in 1995 by founder, Vianna Stibal. Vianna's spiritually directed wisdom can be found in many books, dvd's, webinars and workshops. Theta Healing® is a meditative technique and spiritual philosophy that helps people deeply develop a personal relationship with the Creator. Vianna's first book, *ThetaHealing: Introducing an Extraordinary Energy Healing Modality* published by Hay House, gives many techniques to help with pulling negative beliefs and emotions to make positive change in your life. There are over 500,000 practitioners of Theta Healing® worldwide, in over 150 countries. Phenomenal changes have occurred in the lives of a vast number of people who work with the Energy of All That Is.

Is Theta Healing® the only way? No of course not. Each of us can already do magnificent works. However, we have to remember or re-learn the knowledge that was forgotten. Then release all doubt and believe that we can accomplish incredible tasks as a witness to Universal Energy's Divine Power. We are not the miracle makers if you choose to use that word; we are witnesses to Creator's wonders. It is time for us all to wake up.

As mentioned power behind the intention of downloaded words originate from the Energy of All That Is. I cannot stress this enough. What Is the Energy Of All That Is? It is the One Form that exists in all religions of the planet, known by many names: Spirit, Allah, Jehovah, Yahweh, God, Creator, Source, Great Spirit, Abasi, Hu, Mother- Father- God, Parvardigar, Brahman, Paramatma, Elohim, Chukwu, Olodumare, Ancient of Days, Supreme God, Creator of All That Is, Force, Universal Source and Divine Energy of The Universe to name a few. This energy is the same, the Divine Holy of Holies. It is the expansive power that creates the life force that is continually evolving through each of us. We are each an extension of All That Is.

When we deny love to ourselves or to those we come in contact with in our own lives, we deny Creator, because the Energy of Creation resides in all. There are no exceptions. If we want to evolve to higher levels of vibration or consciousness we should cultivate virtues in our lives. By doing so, we help ourselves, encourage people to do the same, which in turn will help the planet and all on earth as we evolve into a more conscious species. Placing our focus on positive outcomes and happenings around the globe will help life on earth evolve quicker.

It is too easy to be drawn into negative think or give our attention or lip-service to negative happenings we hear on the news, online or from people. We may even be drawn into negative groupthink. This slows positive evolutionary progress. A steady focus on positive changes will help humanity at this time of evolution. Positive group think is unifying and uplifting for life on earth.

Downloads have the remarkable capability to change lives. But you have to get in front of ego and pull the negative beliefs that could impede the success of downloads.

To make changes, we have to give permission or make a conscious effort to approve changes in ourselves. To accept these downloads say yes to allow the energy of the Word to become apart of your energetic physical, spiritual and etheric body. This book is energized with pure intent empowered with energy from Universal Source.

The 112 virtues and over 3000 downloads listed in this book contain variations on the virtuous word to help with precision. It was a stretch finding A to Z virtues and some may lay claim they are not all virtues, but all fall within the definition of morality. So on a couple, I have taken an author's privilege to have a complete alphabetical list.

A virtue is defined as:
- A beneficial quality or trait
- Conformity to a standard of what is considered right
- Moral excellence
- A capacity to act upon something
- One of the hierarchal orders of angels

You may be wondering if you need virtues in your life. When you look at our planet, what do you see? Where do you focus your attention? When you think of humanity, what do you expect? How do you view humanity?

If your mind just considered negative responses to those questions, you have some work to do. Please take no negative feeling from that statement. The power of intention or where you place your focus is extreme. As individuals, cleaning up that which creates blocks in our physical body is the objective. Not looking at the world filled with people and seeing their "stuff." We must create space to heal ourselves and allow space for humanity to do the same.

'Stuff' changes throughout a person's life. Have faith; we can change through our own free will that which we choose. When humanity can appreciate the uniqueness and worthiness of every individual no matter how they are categorized by society and appreciate our planet, we will see significant changes happening all around us. Do we have to wait for that? No, but wouldn't it be wonderful. Groupthink, or mass consciousness is very powerful. Let's see the beauty in all, even if you may think it is hard to find. I assure you, it is there.

So, lets cultivate the virtues. Then help people see their virtues. Want to know more? Look at your astrological natal(birth) chart and see the virtues you were born with and those you need to work on in this life. I will not go into the many values of a natal chart; but it is worth looking into.

❧ Instructions ❧

Each download must be read out loud to receive the intended energy; when you hear it, say "Yes" out loud with gratitude. You can read this to yourself or a group of people saying yes after a section of virtues. You can say yes after each one or wait till a group is read aloud. The reason for each to be spoken or heard is to clarify to the Universe and your rational mind precisely what it is you desire and expect. It is a statement, affirmation, or a belief that you already have it. Focusing on it's mine, instead of I want it, makes a claim to yourself and the Universe it is so.

If you are listening to someone read the downloads or an audiobook, get comfortable, relax, close your eyes and hear the words you are accepting into your energetic field. If you know how to put yourself into the deep meditative theta state, do so. Tune in and feel the energy of the virtues. We all have the ability to shift our energy and work with it. All downloaded words have a specific frequency. The frequency of the virtues, coupled with your intent, benefits your life. If you are reading the list of downloads to yourself, the energetic intention of this book is to provide you the download in the highest and best of ways.

Once you have accepted your downloads you can allow the virtues to reside within or not. Your will can change the course of your life positively or negatively. If you have a mental block or a belief that prevents your download from "being installed" the block will have to be cleared, so the download is successful. Unconscious beliefs can keep you from incorporating them into your energetic field.

How is it done?

When teaching my students, I begin by asking the following question. "Would you like to know on all levels and understand from the highest perspective what it feels like to" I then read the downloads. By agreeing or saying yes to the download you accept it into your body's energetic field this incorporates the words into your physical and etheric bodies.

After I read a list of downloads, I close with the following statement.

"That you know how to, when to, where to, that it is safe and possible for you too, that you can and do so with grace and ease in the highest and best of ways and live your daily life doing this now." This is where you say yes to accept the downloads. "And so it is."

With positive intent we work with the Force of Universal Flow in the highest and best of ways through allowance and gratitude. It is not the human making the changes with downloads it is Creator Of All That Is. Being connected and having faith in All That Is helps the effectiveness of your downloads.

If you would like to receive daily downloads, join thousands of people at COATI+ Robin Coventry on the Facebook group to get your daily downloads. You can also visit COATIEnjoylife on Instagram. COATI+ U is an online school that helps people that are evolving and is located at www.COATIplusU.com if you would like to know more.

⮞List of Virtues⮜

Abundance/Wealth

Acceptance

Accountability

Affability

Appreciation

Assertive

Awe

Beauty

Benevolent

Caring

Communication

Compassion

Confidence

Consideration

Courage

Courtesy

Creativity

Determination

Dignity

Devoted

Eloquence

Empathetic

Enthusiasm

Energy

Erudite

Faith

Fastidiousness

Fidelity

Flexibility

Forgiveness

Friendly

Generous

Gentleness

Giving

Grace

Gratitude

Gregarious	Knowledge
Happiness	Love
Harmonious	Light
Helpful	Loyal
Honest	Magic
Honor	Majesty
Hope	Mercy
Humanity	Modesty
Humility	Noble
Humor	Nurturing
Idealism	Openness
Initiative	Optimism
Innocence	Patience
Integrity	Peace
Intuitive	Perceptive
Intelligent	Perseverance
Joy	Philanthropic
Judicious	Piety
Justice	Protection
Kind	Punctual

Purity	Thankful
Quintessential	Thoughtful
Reliable	Tolerant
Remarkable	Tranquility
Respectful	Truthful
Responsible	Trustworthy
Resilient	Understanding
Restraint	Unity
Righteous	Valiant
Sensitive	Vibrant
Serenity	Vitality
Service	Vivacious
Significant	Wisdom
Sincere	Worthy
Sobriety	Wonderful
Spiritual	Xenoglossy
Tactful	Youthful
Tenacious	
Zealous	

And so we begin…

❧ Abundance/ Wealth ❧

Ample supply of something or more than enough

I am free from want and limitation

I have freedom from want and limitation

I have the success and prosperity of the Divine Mind

I have opulent abundance

I have great abundance

Abundance flows to me

I am a creator of abundance

I have abundance with grace and ease

Abundance flows to me with grace and ease

Abundance comes to me with ease

I know what abundance feels like

I have a beautiful life filled with opulent abundance

I release the fear of being abundant

I release the fear of everyone coming after me if I am abundant

I allow myself an abundant lifestyle

I allow abundance into every facet of my life

I know how to be abundant

I know all things are possible

I am abundant

I am worthy of abundance

I am worthy of wealth

The great bank of the Universe never fails

Creator is the great banker

All is perfect in the great bank

There is an inexhaustible supply of abundance in Creator's Bank

I have infinite abundance

It is safe for me to allow abundance in my life now

I have Creator's definition of abundance

My definition of abundance is the same as Creator's

I understand the difference between abundance and money

I know the difference between abundance and money from Creator's perspective

I deserve abundance now

Creator gives me definitive signs on what to do

I am open to receiving

All doorways are open to my receiving

I am open to receiving great abundance

I can have abundance and money now

I know what it feels like to have abundance and money now

All channels are open to my successful receiving

I am infinitely successful

I have vast reservoirs of wealth

I am always under direct inspiration

I make accurate decisions quickly

I am open to Universal abundance for me

I am open to my Universal perfect life plan

I see my perfect plan with clarity

All my goals and desires are manifest

Creator is my financer

The Universal Bank finances all my desires

I have prosperity

I am fully equipped for the Divine Plan of my life

My abundance manifests in perfect ways

I can have great wealth and abundance now

I know the difference between great wealth and abundance

My perspective is the same as Creator's about great wealth

It is safe for me to allow abundance and great wealth in my life

I know how to allow abundance and great wealth in my life

I deserve great wealth now

I deserve abundance now

I deserve abundance in the highest and best of ways

I deserve great wealth in the highest and best of ways

The Universe is abundant

The Universe has enough abundance for all

There is enough abundance for everyone in the universe

There is enough great wealth for everyone in the universe

There is plenty for all

I am limitless when it comes to great riches

I am limitless when it comes to money

I am limitless when it comes to great wealth

I am limitless when it comes to great abundance

I know what it feels like to have wealth and abundance in my life

I know it's possible to have both wealth and abundance in my life

It is safe for me to be wealthy and abundant

I am a philanthropist

I am a joyful philanthropist

I am a loving philanthropist

I am a generous philanthropist

I know what it feels like to be generous

I have Creator's definition of generous

My definition of generous is as Creator's

I can be wealthy and be generous

I can be abundant and be generous

My wealth never runs out

My abundance never runs out

My wealth is there for me to give when I choose

My abundance is there for me to give when I choose

I accept the generosity of the Universe

The Universe generously gives to me

I am worthy of the Universe's generosity

I know how to accept the Universe's generosity

I know what it feels like to accept the Universe's generosity

The Universe is always generous with me

I am worthy of Creator's generosity

Creator is always generous with me

Creator is always increasing my wealth

Creator makes sure I have enough to give continually if I choose

I know how to accept the generosity of people

I know how to accept the Creator's generosity

I know what it feels like to receive great abundance from Creator

I know what it feels like to receive great wealth from Creator

I know what it feels like to keep great wealth

I know what great wealth feels like

I know what it feels like to have great wealth

I know what it feels like to have great wealth and keep it

I know what it feels like to have great wealth and share

I know what it feels like to share

I know what it feels like for Creator to share with me

I know what it feels like for the Universe to share with me

I know what it feels like for the Universe to share great wealth with me

I know what it feels like for the Universe to provide great wealth to me

I know what it feels like for the Universe to provide great abundance to me

I know what it feels like to have great abundance and wealth

I know what it feels like to have a lot of money doing what I love

I know what it feels like to be wealthy and do what I love

I know what it feels like to have abundance flowing to me

I am worthy of having Great abundance and wealth

I'm worthy of having great wealth

My definition of worthy is the same as Creator's

I have Creator's definition of worthy

I know how to give and to assist all life forms

I know how to teach others how to be wealthy and abundant

Great wealth flows to me

My cellular receptors are open to great wealth and abundance

Every atom in my being knows that it is wealthy

I vibrate wealth and abundance with grace and ease

I know how to be wealthy free from apologizing for it

I know how to manage great wealth

I know what to do with great wealth

My perspective on success and wealth is the same as Creator's

I am wealthy and free from giving it all away

My revenue steams are always increasing

I know how to have a constant flow of revenue

It is safe for me to have a constant flow of revenue

My revenue grows exponentially each day

My wealth is continually growing

My wealth and abundance never runs out

I have plenty to give to my children now

I have plenty to donate now

I have plenty now

I know what it feels like to have plenty

My wealth and abundance survives long after I have died

I have plenty to pass along to my children when I die

I enjoy my wealth while I am alive

I have fun with my wealth while I am alive

I have plenty to give to my children when I am living

A golden opulent perspective radiates throughout and within my life

I am living the Divine Plan of perfection

I am living the Divine Design of health, wealth, love and perfect self-expression

Creator is my unfailing supply of large opulent sums of money

Creator supplies me with unfailing large sums of money quickly under grace in perfect ways.

I have large sums of money with grace

I work a few hours a week

I am beyond being paid by the hour

I am paid large sums of money in the perfect way

My work brings me large sums of money

Large sums of money flow to me with grace and ease in the perfect way

My Divine Bank Account is open for my regular use

I clearly see my full bank account

I clearly see my wallet filled with lots of money all the time with grace.

My savings account is loaded with money

Endless wealth gracefully flows to me in a variety of ways

Endless abundance gracefully flows to me in a variety of ways

I see miracles in my life daily

Miracles are drawn to me daily

I believe in Miracles

I believe the Universe has me aligned with great abundance

I am now on the road of success, happiness and abundance

Opulent abundance flows my way

I am living in the Kingdom of Fulfillment now

I have my own businesses and capable people running them

I surround myself with people that are trustworthy

I connect with my internal gold mine creating abundance with grace

I dwell in the house of abundance forever in my perfect way with ease

Abundance reaches me in the kindest and easiest

I give thanks for my opulent abundance

I give thanks for my infinite abundance

I am grateful for the millions flowing now pouring into my life

Unexpected doors fly open, unexpected channels are free as endless avalanches of abundance are poured upon me under grace and in perfect ways now.

I spend money under direct inspiration wisely and fearlessly, knowing my supply is endless and immediate

I am fearless in letting money go out, knowing Creator is my immediate and endless supplier of my wealth

Money flows to me in the perfect ways continually with ease

I am a savvy investor

I have financial freedom

My supply of money is inexhaustible and immediate and comes to me under grace and in perfect ways

My supply of opulent abundance come to me in perfect ways forever

I am a financial wizard

I know exactly how to invest my millions and billions

My permanent wealth, permanent health, permanent love and permanent happiness is infused by Creator

I am linked with an invisible unbreakable cord to all that belongs to me by Divine Right

Creator's abundant gifts can never be revoked or taken from me

I am constantly connected to the law of abundance

More money is always flowing to me with grace

Creator is the supplier of all I desire

I am grateful for the abundance of life

I am in harmony with Creator's magic

I can make a difference in the world and make money too

I can earn more than I ever dreamed

My ancestors past present and future desires are all fulfilled

My ancestors know what abundance feels like

My ancestors know how to make money wisely

My ancestors made money honestly

My ancestors were taught what abundance is

My ancestors have Creator's definition of abundance

I make money honestly with grace and ease

I know how to help evolving humanity with my money

Divine winds faithfully blow from the North, South, East and West bringing abundance to me.

I am worthy of abundance

I am worthy of wealth

I am wealthy

I am a wealthy person

My family is wealthy

My ancestors were wealthy

My ancestors know what it feels like to be wealthy

I know what it feels like to be wealthy

Wealth flows to me with ease

I am free from all blocks to wealth

I know what wealthy feels like

I know it's safe to be wealthy

I know it's possible for me to be wealthy

I know how to spend my wealth wisely

I know how to invest wisely

I have a wealth mentality

I have an abundantly wealthy mentality

I know what it feels like to be abundant with money

I know what it feels like to have abundant money

I know it safe for me to have abundant money

I know what it feels like to have great wealth

I vibrate great wealth

I vibrate great abundance

I trust the Universe to provide me with wealth now

I received wealth in the highest and best of ways always

Money flows to me with ease

Money constantly flows to me

I am a money magnet

I have all I desire or want

I know how to be a wealthy person

I know how to be an abundant person

It is safe for me to be wealthy and abundant now

I am grateful for my abundance

I am grateful for my wealth

I am grateful that Universe blesses me with great abundance
and wealth

I have Creator's perspective on great abundance and wealth

I allow myself to have Great abundance and wealth

I know what it's like to prosper

I know what it feels like to prosper and be wealthy

I have Creator's definition of prosperity

My definition of prosperity is the same as Creator's

I am prosperous now

I know how to live my life free from the fear of being abundant

I know how to live my life free from the fear of being wealthy

I know how to live my life free from the fear of having money

I know how to live my life free from the fear of being rich

I know how to live with my abundance free from fear

I know how to live with my wealth free from fear

I know how to live with my money free from fear

I know my wealth is mine

I know my abundance is mine

I know my money is mine

It is safe to have wealth and abundance

It is safe for me to have an abundance of wealth

I can be wealthy without working

I know what it feels like to be wealthy without working

I am wealthy and abundant and work when I choose

I am no man's slave

I am not a slave to work

My definition of work is like play

I have fun working when I choose to

I am wealthy in a noble way

I know how to make my money grow exponentially

I am free from those wanting to take my money

I create a positive force with my money

I created a positive force with my great abundance and wealth

I can have it all with grace and ease and in the highest and best of ways

I have balance in my life

I am comfortable loaning people money

I am comfortable giving people money

I am comfortable giving and helping people

I am comfortable donating money

I love to help people

I find great joy in helping people and all life forms

I know how to hire intelligent loving people

I know what it feels like to be intuitive about people

I know what it feels like to be generous

I trust abundant people

I respect abundant people

I know what it feels like for people to be generous with me

I know what it feels like to be accepted and worthy of generosity

I know what it feels like to be in the game of wealth and abundance

I am in the game of wealth abundance

I always play fair with my wealth and abundance

I am always kind with my wealth and abundance

I know how to utilize my wealth and abundance in the highest and best of ways

It is safe for me to have the power of wealth and abundance

I know how to utilize the power of wealth and abundance

I know how to have all my dreams fulfilled

I have all my positive dreams fulfilled

I know how to fulfill the dreams of people

I know how to fulfill the dreams, desires, needs, wants of people in the best of ways

Resources flowed to me with grace and ease

I know what it feels like to manifest create wealth in my life

I know what it feels like to keep great wealth in my life

Creator will bring me anything I choose in the highest and best of ways

I know how to live my life free from want or need

I know how to live and have my wealth free from guilt

I know how to live and have my abundance free from guilt

I have a lot of money and choose how I spend it

My money is my own I am free from being forced to give it away

I know how to have money and pay my taxes

My taxes are all paid

My debts are all paid

I give my money away in and best of ways

I know whom to donate too

I know how to donate and assist with my money

I can create positive opportunities for many people

With my wealth I create positive opportunities for many people

With my great wealth I teach people how to make money too

My great wealth is always replenishing

I have an unlimited great supply of money and abundance

I am wealthy and abundantly blessed

I am blessed with wealth and abundance

The Creator helps me by replenishing my money always

I have all the free time I desire

I enjoy life and help those I choose to enjoy life

I am financially wealthy

My life is abundant in every way

My life is wealthy in every way

I am a wealth maker

Universal abundance is unlimited

I have time to enjoy my money

The sky is just the beginning

There are no limits to my abundance

I am abundant in all positive things

I know and feel that I am in tune with Universal abundance

I am in tune with abundance

My abundance comes with grace and ease

I am debt free

I know how to live my daily life with abundance

I know how to live my daily life being abundant

I am allowed to be debt-free

It is safe for me to be debt-free forever

I earn money while I'm having fun

I know how to make money grow while I'm having fun

There is always plenty for me now

I have a great fortune

I have Creator's definition of a great fortune

My definition of a great fortune is the same as Creator's

I am financially secure

It's safe for me to take time off whenever I choose

I know what it feels like to have complete financial security

It safe for me to have complete financial security

I trust myself to maintain my financial security

I know whom to trust with my finances

I have trustworthy people around me

It is safe to be financially secure

I have Creator's understanding of wealth and abundance

It's possible for me to be famous and have privacy

I know what it feels like to be famous and have privacy

I know what it feels like to be famous free from jealousy

I know what it feels like to be famous and free from negative influences

I know how to use my fame wisely

I know how to be successful in all things

I know how to be successful and free from jealousy

I know what it feels like to be successful and free from people's jealousy

The next download allows you to insert a name

I know what it feels like to be free from the jealousy of_____(name, person)

I know how to respect everyone

I know how to work with powerful people in the highest and best of ways

I know how to choose which powerful people to work with

I know how to create harmony wherever I am

I create harmony with whom I work with

I create abundance with whom I work with

I am allowed to be a powerful harmonious person

I trust myself to create harmony in all I do

I trust myself to create peace in all I do

I draw in all the resources I need when I need them

I know how to draw in the correct people for projects when I need them

I know how to create positive changes with my wealth and abundance

I am comfortable with my own abundance

I am comfortable with the abundance of all people

I am still worthy if people are more abundant than me

I accept that we all have different levels of abundance

The next download allows you to insert a name

It is safe for me to be more abundant than _____
(add name you choose)

I accept that I am abundant

Money flows to me even when I am playing

I do not have to work to have money flowing to me

I allow money to flow to me at all times

I live my life with abundance

❧Acceptance❧

Embracing life on its own terms

The next download allows you to insert a name or title

I accept _____(add any name or title you choose)

I know how, when and where to be accepting

I accept my parents for giving me life

I accept my mother for who she is

I accept my father for who he is

I accept that I am different from my parents

I accept that I am uniquely different

I accept others or people for their differences

I know what it feels like to be accepted by all people

I expect to be accepted by all people

I accept all people for who they choose to be

I am allow to accept whom I choose to be involved in my life

I accept myself

I thoroughly and completely accept myself

I have Creator's definition of acceptance

My definition of acceptance is the same as Creator's

I have Creator's definition of acceptance

I know how to live my daily life with acceptance

I know how to live my daily life being acceptable

It is safe to be accepted by people

I accept that it is safe to _____ (add what you choose)

I accept the decision I have made in this lifetime

I forgive and accept myself for _____ (add what you choose)

I accept and expect people to be _____ towards me (add positive feelings)

I am always accepting of myself

I am comfortable, worthy and always accepting of myself

I accept people for who they are

I live my life with acceptance

I accept that I am a spirit being having a human experience

My acceptance of people is guided by Source

I view all species with loving acceptance

Accountability

Willingness to accept responsibility no matter the outcome

I am accountable

I know what it feels like to be accountable

I know how to live my daily life with accountability

I know how to live my daily life being accountable

I have Creator's Definition of accountability and accountable

My definition of accountability and accountable is the same as Creators

I am comfortable with accountability

I am accountable with grace and ease

I am comfortable being accountable

I am worthy of being accountable

I know what it feels like to be accountable

I understand what accountability means in my life

When I am accountable my life is always wonderful

Being accountable feels wonderful

I allow myself to be accountable

It is safe to be accountable

I am held accountable with love

I am held accountable with kindness

I am held accountable with grace and ease

My accountability is always kind

My accountability is always safe

I accept my accountability

I embrace my accountability with love

My accountability is filled with love

I know how to teach people accountability

I know how to teach people accountable acceptance

I live my life with accountability

I hold my thoughts accountable to a high standard

I hold myself accountable to a high standard of living

Affability

Good natured, friendly and easy to talk to

I have Creator's Definition of affability or affable

My definition of affability or affable is the same as Creators

I am comfortable with people who are affable

I am comfortable being affable

I draw affable people into my life

I know how to live my daily life with affability

I know how to live my daily life being affable

I am worthy of affability

I know what it feels like to be affable

My life is filled with affable people

I am always affable

It is safe for me to live my life with affability

I live my life as an affable person

My affable personality shines

I enjoy being affable

I like living my life with affability

I radiate my affability

I am affable in difficult situations

I teach people how to be affable

I am affable

I am grateful for affable people

I appreciate affability

I know Creator's perspective on affability and mine is the same

I am comfortable with affability'

I am comfortable around affable people

Appreciation

Gratitude for something you like

I have Creator's Definition of appreciation and appreciate

My definition of appreciation and appreciate is the same as Creators

I am comfortable with appreciation

I am comfortable being appreciated

I draw appreciative people into my life

I know how to live my daily life with appreciation

I know how to live my daily life being appreciated

I am worthy of appreciation

I know what it feels like to be appreciated free from ego

I am appreciated

I know how to express appreciation

I appreciate life

I appreciate me

I appreciate _____ (add titles or names of your choice)

I appreciate my _____ (add things about you)

It is safe for me to be appreciated

I like appreciation

I like being appreciated

I know how to appreciate people

I know how to appreciate all people

I feel appreciation for all life

I teach people how to show appreciation

I appreciate you

Appreciation radiates from my soul

Assertiveness

Setting clear boundaries with truth in life

I have Creator's definition of assertiveness

My definition of assertiveness is the same as Creators

I am comfortable with assertiveness

I am comfortable being assertive

I know how to live my daily life with assertiveness

I know how to live my daily life being assertive

I draw assertive people into my life

I am comfortable around assertive people

I respect assertive people

It is safe for me to be around assertive people

I am worthy of assertiveness

I know what it feels like to show assertiveness

I know how to and when to be assertive

I am assertive

I understand assertive people

I appreciate the assertiveness of _____ (add title or name)

❧Awe❦

Deep respect for the Source of life, reverence and wonder

I have Creator's Definition of awe

My definition of awe is the same as Creators

I am comfortable with awe

I know how to live my daily life with awe

I know how to live my daily life being in awe

I am comfortable being in awe

I am worthy of awe

I know what it feels like to be in awe

I am comfortable with awe-inspiring people

I am an awe-inspiring person

Beauty

Something that gives pleasure to the mind and senses

I have Creator's Definition of beauty

My definition of beauty is the same as Creators

I am comfortable with beauty

I am comfortable being a beauty

I am worthy of beauty

I know what it feels like to be beautiful

I am beautiful

I am comfortable being called beautiful

I see my own beauty

I know how to live my daily life with beauty

I know how to live my daily life being beautiful

I am a unique beautiful me

I am allowed to be beautiful

It is safe for me to be beautiful

I am comfortable around beautiful people

I am confident around beautiful people

I allow myself to be beautiful

I am beautiful inside and outside

I am beautiful within and without

I am beautiful to the core

All the cells of my body are beautiful

I like being beautiful

I know that everyone has beauty

I appreciate beauty

I can see the unique beauty of each person I meet

I know how to teach people to see and appreciate life's beauty

Benevolent

Mindset to do what is right or good for people and situations

I am benevolent

I have Creator's definition of Benevolent

My definition of Benevolent and Creators are the same

I have Creator's definition of benevolence

My definition of Benevolence and Creators are the same

I am a teacher of benevolence

I know how to live my daily life with benevolence

I know how to live my daily life being benevolent

I radiate benevolence

I understand what being benevolent feels like

I am a benevolent being

I am a teacher of benevolence

I am worthy of benevolence

I know how to help others be benevolent

I am a benevolent person

I know what it feels like for people to be benevolent towards me

I except benevolence in my life

I accept benevolence from people

I am worthy of benevolence

I am comfortable when people are more benevolent than me

I am safe being benevolent

I know how to teach people to be benevolent

Caring

Feeling or showing concern for others

I am caring

I have Creator's Definition of caring and care

My definition of caring and care is the same as Creators

I am comfortable with caring

I know how to live my daily life with care

I know how to live my daily life being a caring person

I am comfortable being caring

I am worthy of being cared for

I know what it feels like to be caring

I appreciate being cared for

I allow people to care for me

I am comfortable allowing people to care for me

I know how to show people I care

I understand how to be caring

I know what being cared for feels like

I know what showing care feels like

I allow myself to be caring

It is safe for me to be caring

❧Communication❧

Exchanging or conveying information

I am filled with clear communication skills

I am a teacher and communicate clearly

I communicate clearly

I am a communicator

I communicate well with _____ (add names or titles of choice)

I am comfortable with communication

I am a communication bridge

It is safe for me to be a channeler of communication

I am always protected when communicating

I communicate with Creator

I am allowed to communicate directly with Creator

Creator communicates directly with all species

I Communicate through All That Is

I now how to communicate with All That Is

I have clear communication channels with All That Is

I am a positive communicator

I help others to communicate

I am a peaceful communicator

I am a loving communicator

My ancestors were positive communicators

I communicate well in the past, present and future

I know what type of communication to use and when

My forms of communication are many

I communicate clairvoyantly

I communicate empathically

I communicate telepathically

I communicate with and without words

My communicate skills are excellent

I use communication skills in the highest and best ways

I am comfortable communicating with people

I am comfortable communicating with all species

I am receptive for communications from all species

I communicate freely

I communicate knowledge

I am a teacher of positive communication

I teach communication skills

I know how to teach Creator's guidance

Creator gives me guiding communication

I allow Creator's wise communications in my life

I communicate with my real self

My real self gives me wisdom

Love flows through all my communications

I know how to communicate with love

I communicate in the highest and best of ways

I know how to communicate with grace and ease

I am a peaceful communicator

I know how to communicate with each person in my life

I know how to effectively communicate in every situation

My words are clear, decisive, and well placed always

My words are always loving and kind in all situations

I always have the right words to speak and say

My words are accurate in every situation

My words can reach the hearts and minds of people

I know how to communicate the truth in all situations

My words are always truthful

I communicate my ideas with grace and ease

I know when to share my ideas and when to remain silent

I know when to remain silent

I know how to remain silent

I know what it feels like to remain silent

Sometimes the best communication is silent

I know how to listen

I'm an excellent listener

I know how to think about the words I want to say before I say them

I know how to strategically use my words

The right words come to me at the right time

There is wisdom in my words

My words are wise

I communicate wisely

I have excellent communication skills

I am a great speaker

I know how to live my daily life with communication

I know how to live my daily life being a communicator
I am free from the fear of speaking

I know what it feels like to be a great speaker

I know what it feels like to be a desired speaker

I am comfortable speaking in front of thousands of people

I am comfortable sharing my words with thousands of people

My words are in tune with Creator

I speak words that help people heal themselves

I know how to guide people with my words in the highest and best of ways

My words are Creator' Words

I am blessed with uplifting communication

My communication is uplifting for all who hear

I clearly understand all communication from people

I know how to shelter myself from negative communication

I am sheltered from negative communication

I am protected from negative communication

I am protected from unkind words

I am protected from unkind thoughts that people communicate into the Universe

I am comfortable listening to a better communicator than me

I am still worthy even though someone is a better communicator

I know how to reach the hearts of those I communicate with

I know how to communicate clearly for each listener

I teach people how to be a better communicator

Compassion

Deep empathy for suffering of others

I am compassionate

I have Creator's Definition of compassion

My definition of compassion is the same as Creators

I am comfortable with compassion

I have compassion for myself

I have deep compassion for people

I have compassion for all species

I know true compassion

I know what compassion feels like

I know what giving compassion feels like

I know how to give compassion

I know how to live my daily life with compassion

I know how to live my daily life being compassionate

It is safe for me to be compassionate

I am comfortable being compassionate

I am worthy of compassion

I have deep compassion for the earth

I know how to show deep compassion

I know what deep compassion feels like

I am compassionate with grace and ease

I am refreshed by compassion

Compassion knows me

I know what it feels like to be compassionate

I teach people how to be compassionate

I know how to work with the Law of Compassion

I know compassion is one of the greatest virtues and I have it

I am grateful for compassion

I appreciate compassion

I am grateful for compassionate people

I appreciate compassionate people

I know Creator's perspective of compassion an mine is the same

I see compassionate people where ever I travel

I expect humanity to be compassionate to all species

My life is filled with compassionate people

I freely give compassion to all species

I see compassionate hearts everywhere

Confidence

A sense of self- assurance from having faith in life

I have Creator's Definition of confidence & confident

My definition of confidence and confident is the same as Creators

I am comfortable with confidence

I am comfortable being confident

I know how to live my daily life with confidence

I know how to live my daily life being confident

I am worthy of confidence

Confidence knows me

I draw confident people into my life

I know what it feels like to be confident

I am comfortable being around confident people

I have confident people around me

In am confident in _____ (add title of choice)

I know how to be confident without seeming egotistical

I allow my confidence to shine

I am a confident person

I am confident free from ego

I am filled with confidence

I am safe when I am confident

I allow myself to be confident

I am worthy of confidence

I teach people how to have confidence

I am grateful for confidence

I am fortified with confidence at work

I know what I am doing

I appreciate confidence in my self and people

I am comfortable being confident around people who are not

I know Creator's perspective on confidence and mine is the same

I teach people how to be confident

I have confidence that life will continue on earth

I have confidence that humanity is waking up

I am confident that life is improving on earth

I am confident in humanity

I am confident

I am fearless and do not second guess my confidence

❧Consideration❧

Thinking carefully about a decision

I have Creator's Definition of consideration

My definition of consideration is the same as Creators

I am comfortable with consideration

I am considerate

I am considerate towards the earth

I demonstrate consideration in all I do

I am considerate of myself

I am considerate of all species

I am comfortable being considerate

I am worthy of consideration

I know how to live my daily life with consideration

I know how to live my daily life being considerate

I draw considerate people into my life

I know what it feels like to be considerate

I am considerate of people's feelings

I am considerate at work

The next download allows you to insert a name or title

I am considerate with _____(add names or titles)

I like being considerate

I teach people how to be considerate

I live my life with consideration

I demonstrate loving consideration in all I o

My life is filled with consideration

I know what giving loving consideration feels like

I give careful consideration to major life changes

I am aware when people are considerate to me

I appreciate being shown consideration

I appreciate considerate people

I am grateful when people are considerate to me

❧Courage❧

Fear transformed into determination

I have Creator's Definition of courage

My definition of courage is the same as Creators

I am comfortable with courage

I am comfortable being courageous

I know how to live my daily life with courage

I know how to live my daily life being courageous

I draw courageous people into my life when necessary

I am worthy of courage

Courage comes to me with ease

I know what it feels like to be courageous

I am courageous

I am a master of the virtue courage

My courage comes when needed

I know what having courage feels like

I naturally have courage

I teach people how to be courageous

❧ Courtesy ❦

Politeness and gracious good manners

I have Creator's Definition of courtesy and courteous

My definition of courtesy and courteousness is the same as Creators

I am comfortable with courtesy

I am comfortable being courteous

I know how to live my daily life with courtesy

I know how to live my daily life being courteous

I am worthy of courtesy

I am a master of the virtue courtesy

I know what it feels like to be courteous

I have courteous people around me

I know how to live my life showing courtesy to people

I am gifted with courteousness

I appreciate courtesy

I show appreciation when people are courteous to me

I appreciate courtesy

I allow myself to be courteous to people

I am always courteous

I am courteous when I am in hurry

I know how to slow down and show courtesy

I know how to teach courtesy

I am courteous to people

I am grateful when people are courteous to me

I appreciate courteous people

I know Creator's perspective on being courteous and mine is the same

Creativity

Generation of thoughts and ideas of something new

I have Creator's definition of creativity

My definition of creativity is the same as Creators

I am comfortable with creativity

I am comfortable being creative

I am worthy of being creative

I know what it feels like to be creative

I am very creative

I am a master of the virtue creativity

I am grateful for my creativity

I create to help humanity

I am a creative _____ (add title)

I know how to live my daily life with creativity

I know how to live my daily life being creative

I draw creative people into my life

I am allowed to be extremely creative

I know how to express myself in creative ways

I am connected to Source when I am creating

It is safe for me to be creative

I allow myself to create

I know what it feels like to be extremely creative

I always have an outlet for my creativity

I know how to channel my creativity

I teach people to be creative

I am one of Creator's creators

I understand how to be creative in all things

My life is filled with creative people

I know how to teach people to be creative

I am known for my creative abilities

I know how to exercise my creativity

I love creating creatively

I am gifted with creativity

I appreciate my creativity

I appreciate creative people

I have a continuous supply of creativity

I know Creator's perspective on creativity and mine is the same

Determination

Continuing to try to do or achieve something

I have Creator's definition of determination

My definition of determination is the same as Creators

I am comfortable with determination

I am worthy of determination

I am a master of the virtue determination

I know how to live my daily life with determination

I know how to live my daily life being determined

I draw determined people into my life

I know what it feels like to be determined

It is safe for me to be determined

I know how to be determined

I am determined in business

The next download allows you to insert a name or title

I am determined with _____ (add name or title)

❧Dignity❧

Appearing or behaving with serious self-control

I am dignity

I have Creator's definition of dignity

My definition of dignity is the same as Creators

I am comfortable with dignity

I am a master of the virtue dignity

I am comfortable living with dignity

I know how to live my daily life with dignity

I know how to live my daily life being dignified

I draw dignified people into my life

I am worthy of dignity

I know what it feels like to be filled with dignity

I am dignified

I know what dignity feels like

Devoted

Commitment to something you deeply care about

I have Creator's definition of devoted

My definition of devoted is the same as Creators

I have Creator's definition of devotion

My definition of devotion is the same as Creators

I am devoted to living life to the fullest

I understand what devotion is

I am a master of the virtue devoted

I understand what devoted is

I know how to be a devoted person

I know how to commit and be devoted to a cause

I am devoted to self-improvement

I am a devoted person

I am devoted to Universal Love

I am devoted to Creator Of All That Is

I know how to devote my time to what ever I choose

I am lovingly devoted to my spiritual growth

My devotion to my spiritual growth runs deep

I am devoted

I am a devoted teacher

I am a devoted _____ (add title)

I am devoted to Creator

I am allowed to be devoted

Devotion is a powerful active emotion

I know how to live my daily life with devotion

I know how to live my daily life being devoted

I have fearless devotion

I am free from devotional shame

I am free from devotional regrets

I am free from devotional punishment

I am freely devoted

I know how to be devoted

I know when to be devoted to something

I know it is possible to be devoted

I know when to devote my life to something

I know how to and what it feels like to be devoted

The next downloads allow you to insert a name or title

I understand what it feels like to be devoted
to_____ (add name or title)

I know what it feels like to be devoted to_____

It's safe for me to be devoted to_____

I am devoted to what I choose to be devoted too

I am comfortable when people are more devoted than me

I am still worthy when people are more devoted than me

It is safe for me to be devoted to _____

I know what it feels like to be devoted

Eloquence

Powerful, fluent, persuasive, articulate speaking

I have Creator's definition of eloquence

My definition of eloquence is the same as Creators

I am comfortable with eloquence

I am comfortable being eloquent

I am a master of the virtue eloquence

I know how to live my daily life with eloquence

I know how to live my daily life being eloquent

I am worthy of eloquence

I know what it feels like to be eloquent

I am comfortable being eloquent

I am allowed to be eloquent

It is safe to be eloquent

I am an eloquent speaker and am comfortable in front of crowds

I teach people how to be eloquent

Empathetic

Being compassionate and understanding towards peoples situation, feelings and motives

I am empathetic

I am an empathetic listener

I am filled with empathy

I am a master of the virtue empathetic

I know what empathy is

I have Creator's definition of empathic

My definition of empathetic and Creator's is the same

I have Creator's definition of empathy

My definition of empathy and Creator's is the same

 I am an empathetic healer

I am an empathetic teacher

I am an empathetic _____(add titles here)

I teach Creator's Empathy

I know how to and when to be empathetic

My ancestors were empathetic

I am empathetic in the past, present and future

My genetic line is empathetic past, present and future

I know how to live my daily life with empathy

I know how to live my daily life being empathetic

I know how and when to feel empathy

I know what it feels like to be empathetic

I am empathy

I know what it feels like for people to respond empathetically towards me

I know how to receive empathy from others

I can accept when people are empathetic towards me

I allow others to be empathic towards me without being a victim

I am always comfortable when people are more empathetic than me

I am worthy of empathy

Everyone is worthy of empathy

I appreciate empathetic people

I am grateful for empathetic people

⌘Enthusiasm⌘

Exuberance overflowing with eager enjoyment or approval

I have Creator's Definition of enthusiasm

My definition of enthusiasm is the same as Creators

I am comfortable with enthusiasm

I am a master of the virtue enthusiasm

I am comfortable being enthusiastic

I know how to live my daily life with enthusiasm

I know how to live my daily life being enthusiastic

I am worthy of enthusiasm

I know what it feels like to be filled with enthusiasm

I am enthusiastic

I am worthy of being enthusiastic

The next download allows you to insert a name or title

I am enthusiastic about _____ (insert name or title)

My enthusiasm shines

I am allow to shine

It is safe for me to shine enthusiastically

I show enthusiasm free from ego

I am comfortable around enthusiastic people

I am allowed to be enthusiastic

I teach people how to show enthusiasm

I appreciate enthusiastic people

I am grateful for enthusiastic people

Enthusiastic people make life fun

I know how to be enthusiastic

I live life enthusiastically

I know what is feels like to live enthusiastically

I know when to an when not to be enthusiastic

I know when to show enthusiastic support

My enthusiasm is contagious

I am enthusiastic about life

I allow my enthusiasm about life to be unleashed

❧Energy❧

Power derived from Source

I am always connected to Source Energy

I am energy

I am a master of the virtue energy

I am an energetic being

I know how to work with energy

I have Creator's definition of energy

My definition of energy and Creator's is the same

I know all things are energy

I work with Creator's Energy

I am safe working with energy

I am an energy healer

I am an energy instructor

I am full of energy

I radiate energy

Everything is created by and with energy

All That Is is Energy

We are allowed to work with energy

I am an energy worker

I am filled with energy

I always have enough energy to do what I want

I always have energy

I radiate loving energy

I radiate peaceful energy

I know how to live my daily life with energy

I know how to live my daily life being connected to Source energy

I radiate Creator's Energy

I am allowed to radiate energy

I am protected from negative energy

Negative energetic thoughts and words avoid my energetic field

I know how to create positive energy wherever I go

I know how to connect with the Universe in the highest and best of ways

I am in energetic alignment with my higher self

I am in energetic alignment with Source Energy

My chakra energy is open

I know how to use my Heart/Mind energetic connection

I know I am energetically connected to all life

I am a positive energetic influence on earth

My thoughts, words and deeds submit positive energy to the Universe

My body's energetic field radiates joy to all

I am still a worthy person when someone is more energetic than me

I am comfortable in all people's energetic fields

I am accepting of the changes in my energetic field

I know how to work with my energetic field

I know how to work with the energetic field of people

I know how to create within the Universal Energetic Field

I am a part of the Universal Energetic Field

It is safe to be a creator in the Universal Energetic Field

I am always worthy in all my energetic connections with people

My energetic field is in alignment with Creator

I am aligned with the energy of my Higher Self

I teach people how to work with energy

I teach people how to clean up their body's electromagnetic field

❧Erudite❦

Having great knowledge or wisdom obtained by studying

I know how to have an erudite discussion

I am comfortable conversing in an erudite discussion

I have Creator's definition of erudite

I have mastered the virtue erudite

I know how to live my daily life with erudite

I know how to live my daily life being erudite

My definition of erudite is the same as Creators

I know what it feels like to be erudite

I am safe being erudite

Erudite teachers show up when I need them

Erudite people are drawn to me

I appreciate the time it takes to be erudite

I respect erudite people

I accept erudite people into my life

I allow myself to become erudite

I know Creators definition of Erudite mine is the same

❧Faith❧

Belief in the reality of Grace and trust

I have fearless faith contributing joy

My faith is fearless

My faith in Creator is all-powerful

I have faith that the Universe will provide my wishes and desires

I know the Universe has an Amazing Divine Plan for me

I have faith that Divine Order is established in my mind, body and Spirit in all affairs

I have faith I will fulfill my destiny with ease and grace

I have faith that Creator works magic for me

I have mastered the virtue faith

I have Creator's definition of faith

My definition of faith and Creator's is the same

I know what having faith feels like

I am worthy of Creator's magic

We are all worthy of Creator's magic

I have faith In All That Is

I have faith in myself

I know how to live my daily life with faith

I know how to live my daily life being faithful

I understand what faith is

I am allowed to have faith in myself

I have faith in all life forms

I have faith in humanity

I have faith in my family (substitute other names/ titles here)

I have faith

I have strong faith

I have faith that all will work out in the highest and best of ways

I have faith I will accomplish my mission in this lifetime

I am a faithful person

The next download allows you to insert names or titles

I am faithful to _____(add names or titles)

I am still a worthy person when someone is more faithful than I

I am comfortable with my faith

I teach people how to have faith

I know Creator's definition of faith and mine is the same

Fastidiousness

To be in good physical condition

I have Creator's definition of fastidiousness

My definition of fastidiousness is the same as Creators

I am comfortable with fastidiousness

I have mastered the virtue fastidiousness

I am comfortable being fastidiousness

I know how to live my daily life with fastidiousness

I know how to live my daily life being fastidious

I am worthy of fastidiousness

I know what it feels like to be fastidiousness

I am allowed to be fastidious

It is safe for me to be fastidious

I understand what fastidiousness is

I teach people about fastidiousness

I know Creator's perspective on fastidious and mine is the same

≈Fidelity≈

Abiding by an agreement with sacred conviction

I have Creator's definition of fidelity

My definition of fidelity is the same as Creators

I am comfortable with fidelity

I know how to live my daily life with fidelity

I am worthy of fidelity

I know what fidelity feels like

It is safe to have fidelity in my life

I understand what fidelity is

I have mastered the virtue fidelity

I teach people fidelity

I appreciate people who live with fidelity

I am grateful for fidelity

I know Creator's perspective on fidelity and mine is the same

Flexibility

Willingness to try or do something different

I have Creator's Definition of flexibility

My definition of flexibility is the same as Creators

I am comfortable with flexibility

I am comfortable with flexibility

I know how to live my daily life with flexibility

I know how to live my daily life being flexible

I draw flexible people into my life

I am worthy of flexibility

I know what it feels like to be flexible

I am safe being flexible

I know what flexibility feels like

I have mastered the virtue flexibility

I teach people how to be flexible

I am grateful for flexibility in life

I appreciate flexible people

I enjoy being flexible

≪Forgiveness≫

The act of forgiving or letting things go with compassion

I feel forgiven

I know what forgiveness feels like

I have Creator's definition of forgiveness and forgive

My definition of forgiveness and forgive is the same as Creator's

I forgive everyone and everyone forgives me

I am a forgiving person

I call on the law of forgiveness to see past all mistakes and consequences of my mistakes

I am forgiven

I exercise forgiveness in the kindest of ways

I am a forgiver

I am allowed to forgive

I forgive myself

It's time for me to be forgiving of everyone

I know how to forgive

I know what it feels like to forgive

My cells know what it feels like to forgive

I know forgiveness at the cellular level

My cells forgive me for ignoring their health

I release the energy of no forgiveness

I am free from the energy of no forgiveness

My energetic field is freed from no forgiveness

I'm open to forgiveness

I'm willing to forgive

It's safe for me to forgive
It's possible for me to forgive

I know what it feels like to forgive

I know forgiveness is for me

I allow myself to forgive

My energy field feels better when I forgive

Forgiveness shows compassion

I forgive myself

I am allowed to forgive myself

It is safe for me to forgive myself

I forgive me

I forgive I

When it's time to forgive I know how to forgive

Forgiveness is about me

I know how to forgive my father

I know how to forgive my mother

I know how to forgive my sister

I know how to forgive my brother

I forgive my father

I forgive my mother

I forgive my sister

I forgive my brother

I know how to forgive my uncle

I know how to forgive my aunt

I know how to forgive my cousin

I forgive my uncle

I forgive my aunt

I forgive my cousin

The next downloads allow you to insert a name and/or title

I know how to forgive my _____ (insert title)

I know how to forgive _____ (insert name)

I forgive _____ (insert name or title)

It feels wonderful to forgive

I am joyous when I forgive

My spirits soars when I forgive

I am completely safe forgiving anyone

I forgive my government

I forgive my teachers

I forgive myself for being angry

I forgive myself for times when I felt unforgiveable

I forgive myself for seeking revenge

I forgive myself for being unkind to people

I forgive myself for being unkind

I forgive myself for being resentful

I forgive myself for gossiping

I forgive myself for sending negative thought energy to anyone

I forgive myself for causing harm to anyone

I forgive myself for causing harm to anything

I forgive myself for thinking negative thoughts about myself

I forgive myself for thinking negative thoughts about those I love

The next download allows you to insert a name or title

I forgive myself for thinking negative thoughts about

_____

I am worthy of forgiveness

The next download allows you to insert a name or title

_____ is worthy of forgiveness

I can forgive anyone for anything

I can forgive anything

I allow myself to forgive

I am a forgiving person

I know forgiveness

I am worthy of forgiveness

We are all worthy of forgiveness

I forgive my disease

I forgive my injury

I know how to live my daily life with forgiveness

I know how to live my daily life being forgiven

I forgive my eyes

I forgive my bones

I forgive my me

I forgive my _____ (insert body parts)

I forgive all of my organs

I forgive all my body parts

I forgive all systems of my body

The next downloads allow you to insert a name and/or title

It is safe for me to be forgiven by _____

It is safe for me to forgive _____

I am allowed to forgive_____

It is possible for me to forgive_____

I am ready to forgive_____

I know I can forgive_____

I forgive_____ for _____me

It is safe for me to forgive_____
for_____ me

I am free from the feelings of no forgiveness

I release feelings of no forgiveness with ease

I'm ready to release all feelings in my energetic field of no forgiveness

It feels great to forgive

It feels wonderful to forgive

It feels good to forgive

I forgive

I release all no forgiveness held within

I am still a worthy person when someone is more forgiving than me

I am comfortable when someone forgives me

I am comfortable when people forgive me

I am comfortable forgiving

I have mastered the virtue forgiveness

I know Creator's perspective on forgiveness and mine is the same

I am grateful for forgiveness

I appreciate forgiveness

When I forgive someone, I release the negative energy of what I was holding completely from my energetic field

I allow myself to give compassionate forgiveness because I too am worthy of compassionate forgiveness

Forgiveness clears the negative energetic connection I hold against someone

Forgiving people feels very good

It is easy for me to let things go

I forgive people who unknowingly harm me

I forgive people who go out of their way to cause offense

❧Friendly❧

Being kind and helpful to people

I am friendly

I know what friendliness, friend, friendship and friendly feels like

I have Creator's definition of friendliness

My definition of friendliness is the same as Creators

I am comfortable being friendly

I know how to be friendly

I know how to live my daily life with friendliness

I know how to live my daily life being a friend

I am safe being friendly

I know how to protect the secrets of my friends

I keep the confidences of my friends

I am loyal to my friends

I draw friendly people into my life

I know what friends feel like

I believe in friendship

I am comfortable with friends

I know how to be a friend

It is safe for me to be a friend

I know how to cultivate friendship

I teach people how to be a friend

I am able to start new friendships

I know how to start new friendships

I am allowed to have friends

I am worthy of friendship

I am worthy of having friends

I am a friendly person

I have mastered the virtue friendly

I am grateful for friendly people

I am comfortable around friendly people

I know when to be suspicious of friendly people

My intuition shows me my genuine friends

I appreciate friendly people

I have Creator's perspective on friendly people and mine is the same

⋙Generous⋘

Being kind and giving unselfishly

I am generous

I have Creator's definition of generosity

My definition of generosity is the same as Creators

I know how to be generous with people

I am a recipient of generosity

I appreciate generosity

I have mastered the virtue generous

I know what it feels like to be generous

I teach people how to be generous

I accept generosity into my life

I am generous and grateful for opportunities to give

I find new ways to be generous

I am grateful for generous people

I enjoy being generous

I allow myself to be generous

Gentleness

Being kind and having a quiet peaceful nature

I have Creator's Definition of gentleness

My definition of gentleness is the same as Creators

I am comfortable with gentleness

I am comfortable being gentle

I know how to live my daily life with gentleness

I know how to live my daily life being gentle

I am worthy of gentleness

I draw gentle people into my life

I know what it feels like to be gentle

I am safe when I am gentle

I know how to be gentle

I appreciate gentleness

My life is full of gentle people

I am gentle

I have mastered the virtue gentleness

❧Giving❧

Providing love, emotional support or items

I am grateful for opportunities to give

I am a happy giver

I know how to give of my time

I know how to give love

I draw givers into my life

I help people and organizations succeed

I am drawn to those I can help the most with grace

I know how to be a compassionate philanthropist

I am a philanthropist and love giving

I know how to give of myself and my resources

I have an abundance of wealth and know how to give properly

I know that it is safe to give

I am a happy giver

I love giving

I know how to give

I know how to live my daily life giving

I know is it safe to give to all life forms

I give positive energy to all

I give loving energy to all

My real self gives me wisdom

I know how to live my daily life with giving

I know how to live my daily life being a giver

I am a teacher of giving

I am a giver of love

I am a giver of peace

I am a giver of healings

I teach people how to give

I have mastered the virtue giving

I am still a worthy person when someone is more giving than me

I appreciate people's giving

I am comfortable when people give more than me or less than me

I respect giving people

❧Grace❧

Elegance of beauty, movement and expression; Openness to bounties of life and trusting in Creator's Love

I have Creator's Definition of grace

My definition of grace is the same as Creators

I am comfortable with grace

I draw people with grace into my life

I am allowed to have grace

I live life with grace and ease

I know how to and when to live with grace and ease

It is safe for me to live with grace and ease

I am comfortable living with grace

I know it is possible to live with grace and ease

I know how to live my daily life with grace

I know how to live my daily life being grace

I am worthy of grace

I know what it feels like to be filled with grace

It is save to trust in grace

I am filled with grace

I have mastered the virtue grace

I treat people with grace

Life supplies me with grace and ease

I accept the bounty of life with grace and ease

I appreciate grace

I am grateful for grace

I have Creator's perspective on grace and mine is the same

I show grace in difficult times

Gratitude

Feeling appreciation and thanks

I am grateful

I have Creator's Definition of gratitude

My definition of gratitude is the same as Creators

I am comfortable with gratitude

I know how to live my daily life with gratitude

I know how to live my daily life being grateful

I am comfortable being grateful

I draw grateful people into my life

I am grateful for _____ (add name, title or something)

I am worthy of gratitude

I have mastered the virtue gratitude

I know what it feels like to be grateful

I know how to be grateful

I know how to show gratitude

I know what gratitude feels like

I am safe being grateful

❧Gregarious❧

Outgoing, talkative while enjoying the company of people

I have Creator's definition of gregariousness

My definition of gregariousness is the same as Creators

I am comfortable with gregariousness

I am comfortable being gregarious

I know when to be silent or be gregarious

I know how to live my daily life with gregariousness

I know how to live my daily life being gregarious

I am worthy of gregariousness

I know what it feels like to be gregarious

I am gregarious

I have gregarious people around me

I accept gregarious people

I am safe being gregarious

I have mastered the virtue gregariousness

I have Creator's perspective on gregarious and mine is the same

Happiness

Showing pleasure or contentment

I am now deluged with the happiness that was planned in the beginning

I am overflowing with happiness in my life

I am filled with wonderful joy

I have Creator's definition of happiness

My definition of happiness and Creator's is the same

I have Creator's definition of happy

My definition of happy and Creator's is the same

I am happiness

I trust my happiness will continue

I am a master of the virtue happiness

I am harmonious, happy radiant and detached from all fear

Goodness flows to me in an endless stream of happiness

I expect happiness each and every day

I am allowed to be happy

It is safe for me to be happy

I walk the path of happiness every day

All roads I travel are filled with happiness

I am thankful for my permanent happiness

I am grateful for Creator's plan of happiness for me

The Divine Mind allows incorruptible happiness in my life for all time

All the days of my lives are filled with happiness

I draw happy loving kind people to me

I radiate happiness to all beings

I am one with my undivided happiness and love

Creator's unconditional happiness flows to me and radiates out to all beings

I am happy and love everyone

I am happily loveable

I am happy for and love all those in my past

Happiness fills my world

I am happy to be alive

I am a happy _____(use this phrase for all titles)

I am a happy person

I am always happy

I draw happy people into my life

I see the entire world filled with happy people

I know how to live my daily life with happiness

I know how to live my daily life being happy

I can find happiness wherever I am

Happiness always finds me

I have Creator's definition of happiness and mine is the same

I know how to create and teach happiness

I carry happiness wherever I go

My life's journey is filled with happiness

Happy people are drawn to me

I know how to teach everyone to be happy

I am happy for all the lessons of my life

I am happy and grateful for each day

I know how to spread happiness to people

I am comfortable with people's happiness

I am happy for people when they are happy

I am still a worthy person when someone is happier than me

I know Creator's perspective on happiness and mine is the same

I am grateful for happiness

I appreciate happiness

Harmonious

Pleasing and consistently in unison

I have Creator's definition of harmonious

My definition of harmonious is the same as Creators

I am comfortable with harmony

I draw harmonious people into my life

I can create harmony wherever I go

I am comfortable being harmonious

I am worthy of harmony

I know how to live my daily life with harmony

I know how harmony feels

I am a master of the virtue harmony

My chakras are harmoniously aligned with Source

I know how to live my daily life being harmonious

I know what it feels like to be harmonious

I teach people how to live harmoniously

I am grateful for harmony

I appreciate harmony

❧Helpful❧

Making something easier or giving help

I have Creator's definition of helpfulness & helpful

My definition of helpfulness or helpful is the same as Creators

I am comfortable with helpfulness

I am comfortable being helpful

I am worthy of helpfulness

I know how to live my daily life with helpfulness

I know how to live my daily life being helpful

I know what it feels like to be helpful

I am safe being helpful

I am a master of the virtue helpful

I draw helpful people into my life

I am allowed to be helpful

I know how to be helpful

I am a helpful person

I know how to give people the help they need

I have the resources to be helpful to many people

❧Honest❧

Being fair and truthful

I have Creator's definition of honesty

My definition of honesty is the same as Creators

I am comfortable with honesty

I am comfortable being honest

I am worthy of honesty

I know how to live my daily life with honesty

I know how to live my daily life being honest

I know what it feels like to be honest

I have honest people around me

I draw honest people into my life

I live my life with honesty

I am a master of the virtue honesty

My life is filled with honest decisions

It is safe for me to be honest

I am an honest person

I know what honesty feels like

My words are honest and kind

❧Honor❧

A sense of respect for what is right and the character to live it

I have Creator's definition of honor

My definition of honor is the same as Creators

I am comfortable with honor

I am comfortable being honorable

I am worthy of honor

I am a master of the virtue honor

I know what it feels like to be honorable

I know how to live my daily life with honor

I know how to live my daily life being honorable

I draw honorable people into my life

I am an honorable person

I have honor

I know how to be honorable

Honorable people surround me

I live my life with honor

I am safe living with honor

I teach people how to be honorable

❧Hope❦

Optimistically looking to the future with trust and faith

I am hope

I have Creator's definition of hope

My definition of hope is the same as Creators

I am comfortable with hope

I know how to live my daily life with hope

I know how to live my daily life being hopeful

I am comfortable being hopeful

I am worthy of hope

I know what it feels like to be hopeful

I am hopeful

I am filled with hope

I have hope in humanity

The next download allows you to insert a name or title

I have hope in _____ (add titles or names)

I believe in hope

I teach people how to have hope

I live my life with hope

I am safe being hopeful

I allow myself to have hope

No one can destroy my hope

I know how to give people hope

I teach people how to have hope

I know Creator's perspective on hope and mine is the same

I appreciate people with hope

I am grateful for people with hope

My hope is steadfast in difficult times

There is always hope

Hope is a manifestation before it occurs

❧Humanity❦

An attitude of mercy and caring for people

I have Creator's definition of humanity

My definition of humanity is the same as Creators

I am comfortable with humanity

I am comfortable being part of humanity

I have faith in humanity

I know what humanism feels like

I know how to live my daily life with humanity

I have humanity

I feel humanity for all

I know how to live my daily life being humanistic

I believe that humanity is growing more spiritual

I believed that humanity cares about people

I believe in humanity

I know what it feels like to be a part of humanity

I care about humanity

I see humanity growing peaceful

I see all of humanity as happy

Humility

Accepting our lessons and being thankful without boastfulness

I have Creator's definition of humility

My definition of humility is the same as Creators

I am comfortable with humility

I am comfortable being humble

I know how to live my daily life with humility

I know how to live my daily life being humble

I am worthy of humility my life with humility

I am a humble person

I live my life with humility

I am a master of the virtue humility

I know what it feels like to have humility

I am safe living with humility

I know how to live with humility

&Humor&

Ability to perceive, enjoy or express the absurd, comical or what is amusing.

I am humorous

I have Creator's definition of humor

My definition of humor is the same as Creators

I am comfortable with humor

I have a great sense of humor

I am comfortable being humorous

I know how to live my daily life with humor

I draw humorous people into my life

I know how to live my daily life being humorous

I am worthy of humor

I know when to use humor to lighten a moment

I know how to use humor

I am a master of the virtue humor

I know what it feels like to be humorous

I know how to share my humor with people

I appreciate the humor of people

I am allowed to be funny

It is safe for me to have humor in my life

I appreciate humor

I believe in humor

I have a good sense of humor

I know Creator's perspective on humor and mine is the same

I am grateful for humor

It is easy for me to find humor in life

Humor can be found in the most usual and unusual places

Having a sense of humor helps me not take life so seriously

I relax into humor and can laugh at myself

I find fun sharing humor with people

I appreciate those that share humor with me

❧Idealism❧

Having big dreams acting to purse them as if they are possible

I have Creator's definition of idealism & idealist

My definition of idealism is the same as Creators

I am comfortable with idealism

I am comfortable being idealism

I know how to live my daily life with idealism

I know how to live my daily life being idealistic

I am worthy of being an idealist

I draw idealistic people into my life

I know my ideas and dreams are possible

I feel my ideas and dreams are possible

I am safe with my ideas and dreams being possible

I am a creator of big dreams

I have mastered the virtue idealism

I am a creator of big ideas

I help people fulfill their big dreams

My big dreams are possible

I feel as if my big dreams have already happened

I know what it feels like to be idealistic

It is safe being idealistic

I am allowed to idealistic

I have idealistic friends

I teach people how to be idealistic

I know Creator's perspective on idealistic and mine is the same

I am grateful for idealistic thinking

I appreciate idealistic people

❧Initiative❧

Creatively bringing new ideas into the world

I have Creator's definition of initiative

My definition of initiative is the same as Creators

I am comfortable with initiative

I help people see their ability and initiative

I am comfortable having initiative

I am worthy of people's initiative

I know when to show initiative

I know how to live my daily life with initiative

I know what it feels like to have initiative

I am safe using my initiative

I am allowed to have initiative

I allow myself to have initiative

I know when to show my initiative

I appreciate initiative

I am grateful for people who show initiative

I have initiative in _____

❧Innocence❧

Guileless or not guilty, pure, free from harming

I have Creator's definition of innocence

My definition of innocence is the same as Creators

I am comfortable with innocence

I have mastered the virtue innocence

I am comfortable being innocent

I know how to live my daily life with innocence

I know how to live my daily life being innocent

I draw innocent people into my life

I am worthy of innocence

I know what it feels like to be innocent

People see me as innocent

I allow innocence in my life

I am innocent

I believe in innocence

I have Creator's perspective on innocence and mine is the same

Integrity

Keeping faith in our moral ideas and agreements

I have Creator's definition of integrity

My definition of integrity is the same as Creators

I am comfortable with integrity

I am comfortable having integrity

I am worthy of integrity

I have mastered the virtue of integrity

I feel safe and secure in my integrity

I know how to live my daily life with integrity

I know how to live my daily life being integrity

I know what it feels like to have integrity

I draw people with integrity into my life

I walk the walk of integrity

I am integrity

I am allowed to have integrity

I have friends with integrity

I teach with integrity

I draw in people with integrity

I respect integrity

I am comfortable around people with integrity

I play the game of life with integrity

I have Creator's perspective on integrity and mine is the same

I appreciate integrity

I am grateful for integrity

I am grateful of people of integrity

I can hold fast to my integrity in difficult times

I live my life as a person with integrity

I can teach what integrity is so people understand

❧Intuitive❧

Instinctive feelings based on a person's truth

I am intuitive

I have Creator's definition of intuitive

My definition of intuitive is the same as Creators

I am intuitive around all species

My intuition is strong

I am in touch with my gut feelings

I know how to sense when something is right or wrong

I am an intuitive being

I have mastered the virtue intuitive

My intuition guides me daily

My ancestors were intuitive

I am intuitive past, present and in the future forever

I am an intuitive creator

I trust my intuition

My intuition grows stronger each day

I am intuitive in every way

I am an intuitive teacher

It is safe to be intuitive

I am an intuitive person

I am an intuitive _____ (add title)

I am an inspirational intuitive person

I draw in intuitive people

I have an intuitive energetic field around me

I work with my intuition to grow stronger

I know we are all intuitive

I know how to live my daily life with intuitiveness

I know how to live my daily life being intuitive

I know how to use my intuition wisely

I draw intuitive people into my life

I know when to respond quickly to my intuition

It is safe to be an intuitive person

My intuition guides me well

Each day and in everyway I trust my intuition

I am still a worthy person when someone is more intuitive than me

I allow my intuitive abilities to fully develop

I know what being intuitive means

My intuition grows more attuned to All That is Each Day

My intuition is keen and guides me well

I hear my intuition clearly

I trust my own intuition

Intuition guides me everyday

I see my intuition as a guide to my life

I am clear to the guidance of my intuition

I have Creator's perspective on intuition and mine is the same

I am grateful for my ever-increasing intuition

My intuition always serves me when I need to know

I appreciate people with a developed intuition

I am comfortable around people with strongly developed intuition

I am intuitive

Intelligent

Ability to acquire and apply knowledge and skills

I am intelligent

I am an intelligent being

I have Creator's definition of intelligent and intelligence

Creator's definition of intelligent and/or intelligence is the same as mine

I am in complete alignment with Creator's Intelligence

I am an intelligent teacher

I am an intelligent person (substitute other titles here)

I walk in intelligence

I have mastered the virtue intelligence

My life is filled with intelligent people

I draw in intelligent people

I radiate intelligence

It is safe to be intelligent

I teach intelligence

I am allowed to be intelligent

I am allowed to be more intelligent than my
_____(add what you choose)

I accept my intelligence

My intelligence is free from egoic interference

I am an intelligent person with humility

I have an all-knowing intelligence

I know what it feels like to be intellectually intelligent

I am an intellectual person

I know how to live my daily life with intelligence

I know how to live my daily life being intellectual

I am safe being an intellectual person

I love being an intellectual person

I use my intelligence wisely

I know how to listen and apply my intelligence where I should

I know what it feels like to be an intelligent person

I am an intelligent person

I am connected to the Intelligence of All That Is

I am comfortable around intelligent people

I am comfortable when someone is more intelligent than me

I am safe when someone is more intelligent than me

I am still a worthy person when someone is more intelligent than me

Joy

A blissful feeling of peace and happiness

I am a joyful giver

I am joy

I have Creator's definition of joy and joyful

My definition of joy and joyful is the same as Creator's

I know what joy feels like

I am joyful for my life

I am filled with Creator's Joy

I know Creator's Joy

It is safe for me to be joyful

I know how to live my daily life with joy

I know how to live my daily life being joyful

Joy is my Bliss

I am blissfully joyful

I spread joy

I accept great joy into my life

I am a joyful person (use this phrase for all titles)

I am joy filled

I am filled with joy past, present and future

I am genetically filled with joy

My ancestors were joyful people

My ancestors spread joy

I inherited joy from my ancestors

My cells are joyful

My body is joyful

My energetic field is joyful

I am joyful

My heart radiates joy to all

I know how to spread joy to all life forms

I am allowed to be joyful, joyous and/or filled with joy

I am comfortable with people's joy

I am worthy of joy

I am still worthy of joy when people are joyful

I can participate in people's joy

I love seeing joyful people

I know joy when I see it

I feel the warmth of joy

I feel the bliss of joy

I know what joyful bliss feels like

I am joyfully blissful

I have Creator's definition of Joyful Bliss

My definition of joyful bliss is the same as Creator's

My heart unfurls with joyful bliss

I am alive and filled with joy

I know how joy feels in my life

My life is filled with joy

My heart sings a joyful song

How to and what it feels like to understand the joys of Living

I know what it feels like to have joy in my life

I am allowed to have joy

I am allowed to be joyful

I am allowed to feel joy inside

I give myself permission to experience joy

I am joyful

My life is joyous

I keep my inner joy when around those who are joyless

I know who to spread joy

I radiate joy

Joy is an emotion and I feel it on a regular basis

I am joyful free from the fear of loosing my joy

I know life is meant to be filled with joy

All atomic particles in my body live in joy

My organs are joyful

My bodily systems are joyful

I am a master of the virtue joy

I know Creator's perspective on joy and mine is the same

I appreciate joyful people

I am grateful for the feeling of joy

I am grateful for joyful people

Judicious

Showing good sense, wisdom and discretion avoiding trouble

I have Creator's definition of judiciousness

My definition of judiciousness is the same as Creators

I am comfortable being judicious

I know how to live my daily life with judiciousness

I have mastered the virtue judicious

I know how to live my daily life being judicious

I am comfortable with judicious people

I am worthy of being judicious

I know what it feels like to be judicious

I appreciate judiciousness

I am grateful for judiciousness

I know Creator's perspective on being judicious and mine is the same

I am judicious with my life

❧Justice☙

Using laws to fairly judge and or punish lawbreakers

I have Creator's definition of justice

My definition of justice is the same as Creators

I am comfortable with justice

I am comfortable within the justice system

I am worthy of justice

I know how to live my daily life with justice

I know how to live my daily life being just

I radiate justice

I have mastered the virtue justice

I know what it feels like to give justice to people

I know how to give kind fair justice

I know what it feels like to respect the justice system

I know how to respect the justice system

I know how to see through corrupt justice

I am at peace with justice

I can remain calm and at peace when justice decisions are made

I know how to interpret justice

I know how to help people understand justice

I know how to teach people to be calm with justice

I know how to teach people to relax with justice

I am calm with justice

I am at ease when I hear about justice

I can relax when I see justice

I know I am not the enforcer of justice

I know that it is what it is

I remain calm when I see injustice

I appreciate justice

I am grateful for justice

Kind

Showing compassion that brings happiness

I am kind

I have Creator's definition of kind

My definition of kind is the same as Creator's

I have Creator's definition of kindness

My definition of kindness is the same as Creator's

I know what kindness feels like

I am a kind person

I have mastered the virtue kind

I radiate kindness

I am kind to all I meet

I know what kindness feels like

I know how to be kind

I know I can be kind

My ancestors were kind

I know what it feels like to be kind

I am kind in the past, present and future

I am kindness

Kindness follows me around

My energetic field is full of kindness

People like being kind to me

I know what it feels like when people are kind to me

Kind words are spoken by me

My ancestors spoke kind words

My entire genetic line is kind

My frequency includes compassionate kindness

I spread kindness to all people

I treat all people with kindness

Kindness radiates from me

I am kind to all species

I am kind-hearted

I am known for being kind hearted

I have Creator's definition of Kind-Hearted

My definition of kind-hearted is the same as Creator's

I am worthy of kindness

I know how to live my daily life with kindness

I know how to live my daily life being kind

I am comfortable when people are kind to me

I am allowed to be treated kindly

I am worthy of people's kindness

I expect kindness from all people

My world is filled with kind people

I am kind to all people I meet

I allow kindness to fill my life

I know what it feels like to speak words of kindness to all

I lovingly promote kindness to the world

Kindness flows to me from all directions

᠀Knowledge᠀

Practical understanding of a subject

I am knowledge

I have knowledge

I have Creator's definition of knowledge

My definition of knowledge is the same as Creators

It is safe to have knowledge

It is safe to share knowledge

All species have knowledge

I am knowledgeable

I have mastered the virtue knowledge

Knowledge fills my world

I know what to do with my knowledge

I have knowledge of past, present and future lives

I am always filled with knowledge

I am a teacher of knowledge

I draw knowledgeable people into my life

Knowledge arrives exactly when I need it

I radiate knowledge

I have the Knowledge of Creator

Creator always refreshes my knowledge

Creator gives me knowledge of life

I know how to live my daily life with knowledge

I know how to live my daily life being knowledgeable

I know how to communicate my knowledge

My life is filled with knowledge of the mysteries of life

I remember ancient knowledge long forgotten

The knowledge of ancient wisdom fills my soul

I know how to use ancient knowledge correctly

I know how to understand ancient knowledge

I understand ancient knowledge

Ancient knowledge flows to me

I am filled with the wisdom of ancient knowledge

It is safe for me to learn and know ancient knowledge

I know ancient knowledge

I understand how to use ancient knowledge

I see ancient knowledge as the tool that it is

I understand ancient knowledge completely

The wisdom of ancient knowledge flows to me

Light

Natural agent that stimulates sight and makes things visible

I am grateful for sunlight flowing into my life

I am grateful for Divine Light flowing into my life

I am Light

I am Divine Light

Divine Light shines on me

I radiate Divine Light

Universal Energy is Divine Light

Creators Divine Light flows to me past, present and future

I know what Divine light feels like

My body radiates Divine Light

I glow in the dark

I am safe glowing in the dark

I bring light to dark places

I am an illuminator

I am accelerating the mastery of Divine Light

I am a light being

I have Creator's definition of light

My definition of light is the same as Creators

I am a being of light

I am allowed to radiate Creator's Light

I am Creator Light

It is safe for me to radiate Creator' Light

I have intimate knowledge of Creator's Light

I glow with Creator's Light

I radiate light

I am filled with Creator's Light

Creator's Light fills me

It is safe to be filled with Creator's Light

I have an abundance of Light

I am Light

I know how to live my daily life with light

I know how to live my daily life being a light being

I bring Light wherever I go

I have light past present and future

I am future Light

I am a Light glowing in the past

I am a Light glowing in the present

I am a Light glowing in the future

I am a Light glowing wherever I am

I am Light shine

I shine Light

My Light shines

My Light never goes out

I am a bringer of Light

I am a Light bearer

I spread Creator's Light

I am a fearless Light worker

I appreciate the Light

I am grateful for the Light

I know Creator's perspective on Light an mine is the same

Love

The heart connection between hearts or deep attraction for something

I love myself

I love all species on earth

I know what love feels like

I am always connected to Creator's Love

I know what Creator's Love feels like

I know what it feels like to be loved by all species

I know what it feels like to be love by family

I am loved by family

I radiate love

I have mastered the virtue love

I have Creator's definition of love

My definition of love is the same as Creators

My ancestors were loved by their family

I have love past, present and future

I am surrounded by love

I am a communicator of love

I know how to communicate love

My world is filled with kind people

I am a teacher of love

Creator gives me love

There is always enough love to share

The planet is filled with Love

I live on a loving planet

All species are filled with love

All species know love

I know how to live my daily life with love

I know how to live my daily life being loved

I am allowed to radiate love

It is safe to be loved

I love all species

My frequency contains compassionate love

My genetic line is full of love

My ancestors were and are loving people

I am love in the past, present and future lives

I know how to receive and give love

It is safe for me to give and receive love

My ancestors gave and received love

It is possible to always show love

I know how to always show love

Love is the strongest force in the universe

I am embraced by love

I always love

I know what it feels like to receive love from

_____

I feel loved every day of my life past, present and future

My entire ancestral line feels loved in past, present and future

The world is filled with love

I see the world filled with love

I teach people how to love

I know Creator's perspective on love and mine is the same

I am grateful for love

I appreciate love

I appreciate loving people

I am grateful for loving people

I align myself with loving people

Loving people are drawn to me

I allow myself to feel loved

❧Loyal❧

Quality of showing firm support or alliance

I am loyal

I know what loyalty feels like

I know how to be loyal

I am a loyal person

I am loyalty

I know how to live my daily life with loyalty

I know how to live my daily life being loyal

I radiate loyalty

I know what loyalty feels like

I am safe being loyal

My life is filled with loyal people

I know what being loyal means

I know loyalty

I understand what loyalty is

I understand how to be loyal

I know it is safe for me to be loyal to a cause

Loyal people surround me

The next download allows you to insert a name or title

I am loyal to _____ (add name, title or organization)

I appreciate loyalty

I am grateful for loyalty

I know Creator's perspective on loyalty and mine is the same

Loyal people are drawn to me

I know who to, when to and how to give my loyalty to people

I am comfortable around loyal people

I accept loyal people without expecting betrayal

I enjoy being around loyal people

I feel safe around loyal people

I am a loyal _____ (insert title of your choice)

❧Magic☙

Influencing events using mysterious or supernatural means

I am Magic

I know what Magic is

I am filled with Creator's Magic

I know what it feels like to be magic

It is safe for me to be magic

I have Creator' definition of magic

My definition of magic is the same as Creator's

It is a magical world

My world is filled with magic

Life is filled with magic

I live with magic in my life everyday

I have magic in my life everyday

I am allowed to have magic in my life everyday

It is safe to believe in magic

I believe in Creator's Magic

I know magic is possible

I have magic

I am magical

My ancestors were magic

My ancestors were in touch with their own magic

I am magic past, present and future

I spread magic to all

I am in touch with earthy magic

I draw magic people into my life

I see the magic of creation

I see magic wherever I look

I draw positive, loving magical beings into my life when I choose

It is safe for me to draw magical beings into my life

I am in touch with Universal magic

Magic radiates from me

I am a magic maker

I am a magic person (can substitute all titles here)

I am embraced by loving magic

I create magical experiences

I create magic in my life

I am a teacher of magic

I know how to live my daily life with magic

I know how to live my daily life being magical

I teach all about their own magic

I expect the magic of miracles

Miracles are Divine magic

I see miracles in my life each day

Each human is endowed with their own magic

I know how to respect the magic of everyone

I respect magic

I respect the Divine gift of magic

It is safe for all people to utilize their own magic

I know we are all magical

I am free from any fear of magic

I am free from ancestral fears of magic

It is safe to be magical

I am a magic sage

I know how to use magic in the highest and best of ways

My magic shines to all that experience it

Magic is my friend

Life is filled with magic each and everyday of life

Magic fills the Universe

Learning magic is a universal right

I know how to weave magic into life

I know Creator's perspective on Magic and mine is the same

I am grateful for magic

I appreciate magic

I appreciate magical people in my life

I am fearless around magic

I am free from false beliefs about magic

We all have magic capabilities

I am comfortable with my magic

I am comfortable with the magic of people

I am free from being jealous of someone that is more magical than I am

I allow space for the magic of all people

Majesty

Impressive dignity never cheating anyone

I have Creator's Definition of majesty

My definition of majesty is the same as Creators

I am comfortable being majestic

I draw majestic people into my life

I know how to live my daily life with majesty

I know how to live my daily life being majestic

I radiate majesty

I am worthy of majesty

I know what it feels like to be majestic

I understand majesty

It is safe for me to be majestic

I draw majestic people into my life

The next download allows you to insert a name or title

I am majestic with _____ (insert name and title)

I am comfortable being around majestic people

❧Mercy❧

Compassion shown to offenders by someone administering justice

I have Creator's definition of mercy

My definition of mercy is the same as Creators

I am comfortable with mercy

I am comfortable being merciful

I am comfortable giving mercy

I have mastered the virtue mercy

I am worthy of mercy

I draw merciful people into my life

I know how to live my daily life with mercy

I know how to live my daily life being merciful

I know what it feels like to be merciful

I am safe showing mercy

I radiate mercy

I know what it feels like to give mercy to people

I know mercy

I freely give mercy

I am worthy of mercy

I understand mercy

The next download allows you to insert a name or title

I show mercy to _____ (add name or title)

I know how and when to be merciful

I am always shown mercy

I allow mercy into my life

I am grateful for mercy

I appreciate mercy

I know Creator's perspective of mercy and mine is the same

Modesty

Freedom from vanity or conceit also moderate dress

I have Creator's definition of modesty

My definition of modesty is the same as Creators

I am comfortable with modesty

I have mastered the virtue modesty

I am comfortable being modesty

I know how to live my daily life with modesty

I know how to live my daily life being modest

I radiate modesty

I draw modest people into my life

I am worthy of modesty

I know what it feels like to be modest

I am comfortable around modest people

I have modest people in my life

I am a modest person

I know how to be modest

❧Noble❧

*Having high moral standards and faith with our true value as
spiritual beings.*

I have Creator's definition of Noble

My definition of noble is the same as Creator's

I have Creator's definition of Noble-Minded

My definition of noble-minded is the same as Creator's

I am safe when I am noble

I have mastered the virtue noble

I draw noble people into my life

I know how to live my daily life with nobility

I know how to live my daily life being noble

I radiate nobility

I am still worthy when I see noble people

I am safe being noble

I know how and when to be noble

I am surrounded by noble people

Noble people fill my world

I am comfortable with noble people

I am a noble person

I am a noble-minded person

I am comfortable with noble-minded people

All people are worthy of nobility

I am grateful for noble people

I appreciate noble people

I know Creator's perspective on Noble and mine is the same

❧Nurturing❧

Quality of *desiring another to grow or learn*

I have Creator's definition of nurturing

My definition of nurturing is the same as Creators

I am comfortable with nurturing

I am comfortable being nurtured

I am worthy of nurturing

I have mastered the virtue nurture

I know how to live my daily life with nurturing

I know how to live my daily life being nurtured

I know what it feels like to be nurtured

It is safe for me to be nurtured

I know how to nurture people

I am a nurturing _____ (add title)

I know how to kindly nurture people

I can nurture people without a big fanfare

I am a skilled nurturer

I know how to be a nurturer without smothering a person

I know how to let go as a nurturer

I am a balanced nurturer

I know when to and when not to nurture

I appreciate nurturers

I am grateful for nurturers

I know Creator's perspective on nurturing and mine is the same

I allow people to nurture me

I teach people how to be nurturers

❧Openness❧

Willing to consider what people have to say like new thoughts and ideas.

I am open to new ideas

I am open for _____ (whatever you choose)

I have Creator's definition of openness

My definition is the same as Creators

I know how to live my daily life with openness

I know how to live my daily life being open

I am comfortable with openness

I am open to change

I am allowed to be open with people

I welcome openness in communication

I am allowed to exercise openness in life

I appreciate openness

I am grateful for openness

I know Creator's perspective on openness and mine is the same

᠖Optimism᠖

Positive cheerful outlook

I am optimistic

I have Creator's definition of Optimism

My definition of optimism is the same as Creator's

I have Creator's definition of Optimistic

My definition of optimistic is the same as Creator's

I am safe being optimistic

I radiate optimism

I have mastered the virtue optimism

I face each day with optimism

I am allowed to be optimistic

The next download allows you to insert a name or title

I am allowed to be optimistic when I am around
_____ (insert name or title)

I am always optimistic

I draw optimistic people into my life

I know how to live my daily life with optimism

I know how to live my daily life being optimistic

I know how and when to be optimistic

I am surrounded by optimistic people

Optimistic people fill my world

I am worthy of optimism

I am comfortable being around optimistic people

I know what it feels like to be optimistic

The world is full of optimism

I know what optimism feels like

I trust my optimism

I have optimism

I know what optimistic feels like

I am always optimistic

Optimism flows to the world

I am filled with optimism each day

I am optimistic about humanity

I am grateful for optimism

I appreciate optimism

Patience

Waiting peacefully for things to turn out right

I am patient

I know what it feels like to have patience

I have Creator's definition of patience

My definition of patience is the same as Creators

I am allowed to have patience

I have mastered the virtue patience

It is safe for me to have patience

I know how to live my daily life with patience

I know how to live my daily life being patient

My life is filled with patient people

I am comfortable being patient

I radiate patience

I know what it feels like to be patient

I expect people to exercise patience with me

᪥Peace᪥

Inner calm and tranquility

I am at peace with the world and myself

I am a bearer of peace

Peace radiates through my life and into all beings

I bring peace wherever I go

Peace fills my world

I have mastered the virtue peace

I am a peacemaker

My body knows what peace feels like

My body knows how to send love and peace into the world

I radiate peace

It is safe for me to live in peace

It is safe for me to be a peacemaker

I spread peace and love

I allow peace into my life

I walk in peace

My body is a peaceful body

I release all things from my life that are not of peace and love

I know how to walk in peace

I am peace

I am peacemaker

I am aware of peace on all levels

I am peace past present and future

I am filled with the joy of peace

I am a teacher of peace

I teach peace

I know how to talk about positive actions

I think positive thoughts of peace

I focus my life on peace for all

I teach peace

My words are peaceful

My mind is peaceful

The energetic field of my body is peaceful

I am Creating peace wherever I go

Peaceful people associate with me

I see peace and love in all people

I know how to spread the word of peace

My live is filled with peace

I go in peace

My past, present and future is in peace

My genetic tendencies are peaceful

My ancestors are peacemakers

My ancestors created peace and love

My ancestors were blessed with peace and love

My cells speak of peace and love

My body is filled with peace and love

My body knows what peace and love feels like

My planet is a peaceful planet

I live in the beauty of peace

I live in a peaceful world

I enjoy peace

I know how to live my daily life with peace

I draw peaceful people into my life

I know how to live my daily life being peaceful

I enjoy living a peaceful life

I can live my life free from conflict

I am conflict free

I am accepted wherever I go

I am accepted wherever I have been

I am safe living with peaceful acceptance

I am allowed to live in peace

I am free from fighting

I am free from war

I am free from chaos

I am free from anger

I am free from sorrows of war

I am free from being cast into the battles of people

I see people as peacemakers

I am associated with peacemakers

I am a living peacemaker

I am at peace when people around me are not

I am comfortable living in peace

I see the world filled with peace-lovers

I am comfortable around peace-lovers

I am comfortable being called a peace-lover

I am safe being a peace-lover

I am a worthy peace-lover

We are all worthy of peace

I am a fearless lover of peace

I know that Creator accepts me as a peace-lover

I accept me as a peace-lover

I know what peace feels like

I feel like peace

I am peaceful

I have Creator's definition of Peacemaker, Peace-lover and Peaceful

My definition of Peacemaker, Peace-lover and Peaceful are the same as Creator's

I know how to show people with _____ (insert a negative emotion) peace

I live on a peaceful earth

I live in a peaceful universe

I appreciate peace

I am grateful for peace

All species should have peace

I have Creator's definition of peace and mine is the same

I know Creator's perspective of peace and mine is the same

I expect peace in my life

I expect peace on earth

Perceptiveness

Clarity of vision, understanding accurately or intuitive discernment

I am perceptive

I have Creator's definition of perceptiveness

My definition of perceptiveness is the same as Creators

I am a perceptive person

I have mastered the virtue perceptiveness

I know how to live my daily life with perceptiveness

I know how to live my daily life being perceptive

I am allowed to be perceptive

I draw perceptive people into my life

I know how to be perceptive

It is safe for me to be perceptive

I understand my own perceptiveness

I allow myself to be perceptive

My perceptiveness is well evolved

I am comfortable with peoples perceptiveness

I know what it feels like to be perceptive

My perceptiveness continues to be refined

My life is filled with perceptive people

I appreciate perceptiveness

I am grateful for perceptive people

I know Creator's perspective on perceptiveness and mine is the same

Perseverance

Steadfastness when pursuing goals no matter how long it takes

I have perseverance

I know what perseverance is

I know how to live my daily life with perseverance

I have mastered the virtue of perseverance

I know how to live my daily life being perseverant

I have Creator's definition of perseverance

I know what perseverance feels like

I persevere

I draw persevering people into my life

My definition of perseverance is the same as Creator's

I see humanities perseverance

I know what it feels like to persevere

I appreciate perseverance

I am grateful for perseverance

❧Philanthropic❧

Voluntary giving or promotion of a species or person's welfare

I have Creator's definition of philanthropic

My definition of philanthropic is the same as Creators

I am comfortable with philanthropy

I am comfortable being philanthropic

I am worthy of philanthropy

I know how to live my daily life with philanthropy

I know how to live my daily life being philanthropic

I know what it feels like to be philanthropic

I am grateful for being a philanthropist

I know how to work with philanthropists for the greater good

I draw philanthropists into my life

I am a philanthropist

I have mastered the virtue philanthropic

I know how to show gratitude to philanthropists

I know who to help and when

I know how to help people

My donations make a difference in the world

My volunteering makes a difference in the world

I see who needs help and help them

I get accurate information on who needs assistance

I know how to make a plan to use my money wisely

I am talented at finding people to give money to

I have an honest team to help me with my philanthropic ventures

I am grateful for philanthropic people

I appreciate philanthropic people

I am comfortable around philanthropic people

I know Creator's perspective on being philanthropic and mine is the same

❧Piety❧

Humble devotion to a high idea

I have Creator's definition of piety

My definition of piety is the same as Creators

I am comfortable with piety

I have mastered the virtue piety

I am comfortable being pious

I know how to live my daily life with piety

I know how to live my daily life being pious

I am worthy of piety

I know what it feels like to be pious

I draw pious people into my life

I am surrounded with pious people

I know what being pious feels like

I know what piety feels like

I appreciate piety

I am grateful for pious people

Protection

Preventing harm or suffering

I have an infinite level of protection always

Everything that I have, love and cherish is always protected

I am free from parasites and those that want to use me

I am free from all parasitical people

I am free from all parasites

I know how to live free from users

I know how to live parasite free

I release all parasites in my life

It feels great to be parasite free

I am allowed to live free of parasites

I give myself permission to live parasite free

I know what to do to live parasite free

My mind is free from dwelling on parasites

My energetic field is free from drawing in parasites

I am safe from all parasites

I am free from parasites in my paradigm

My reality is parasite free

It is safe to live parasite free

I am free from controlling tendencies of parasites

I am free from being controlled by parasites

My body is repulsive to parasites

My energetic field is repulsive to parasites

I know how to love parasites away

I am free from being host to parasites

My body expels all parasites

I am free from being a slave to parasites

I am safe from all harm

I am always protected from _____ (fill with words)

I am surrounded by protective angels

I am surrounded by Creators protection

I am protected from evil

I have mastered the virtue of protection

I know how to live my daily life with protection

I know how to live my daily life being protected

I have Creator's definition of protection

My definition of protection is the same as Creator's

I know what it feels like to be protected

I know the safety of protection

I am always safe from harmful people

I am always safe in unfamiliar situations

I am always protected in unfamiliar situations

I am protected from all that wish to cause harm

My life is protected from all words or harmful thoughts

Harmful thoughts and words never reach my energetic field

I am safely protected from evil

I allow myself to be protected

I feel safely protected

I know who to protect myself

I have common sense when it comes to protecting myself and those I love

I know Creator's perspective of protection and mine is the same

I know when I should be protected

I am grateful for angelic protection

I allow myself to be protected

Punctuality

Habit or quality of being on time

I have Creator's definition of punctuality and punctual

My definition of punctuality and punctual is the same as Creators

I am always punctual

I know how to live my daily life with punctuality

I know how to live my daily life being punctual

I know the importance of punctuality

I draw punctual people into my life

I have mastered the virtue of punctuality

I am always on time

I know how to respect the time of people

I know what it feels like to be on time

I make plans to be on time

I still to the plan to be on time

I arrive on time

I am known for my punctuality

I know how to be punctual

It is safe for me to be punctual

I am worthy of punctuality

People in my world are punctual

Purity

Physical and spiritual cleanliness

I know what it feels life to be pure

I am pure

My life is filled with purity

I know how to live my daily life with purity

I know how to live my daily life being pure

It is safe for me to life with purity

I draw pure people into my life

I have Creator's definition of purity

My definition of purity is the same as Creators

I am comfortable with purity

I am spiritually pure

I know Creator's perspective of purity and mine is the same

I appreciate purity

I am grateful for purity

I see the waters of the earth and my body basking in purity

❧Quintessential❧

Representing the most perfect example of class or quality

I am a quintessential human

I am a quintessential _____ (add any title)

I quintessentially know what to do

I am safe being quintessential

I have mastered the virtue quintessential

I know how to live my daily life being quintessential

I have Creator's definition of Quintessential

My definition of quintessential is the same as Creator's

I have Creator's definition of Quintessentially

My definition of quintessentially is the same as Creator's

I am the quintessential self

I AM a quintessential creator

I am worthy being quintessential

I am comfortable being around quintessential people

❧Reliable❧

Being dependable and taking responsibility with trustworthiness

I am reliable

I have Creator's definition of reliable

My definition of reliable is the same as Creators

I am a reliable person

I know how to live my daily life with reliability

I know how to live my daily life being reliable

Reliable people surround me

I have mastered the virtue reliable

I draw reliable people into my life

I am safe being reliable

I see people of the world as reliable

I know how to be reliable

I know when and how to be reliable

I believe in being reliable

I radiate reliability

Remarkable

Worthy of attention

I am a remarkable person

I know how to be remarkable

It is safe to be remarkable

I draw remarkable people into my life

I am allowed to be remarkable

I allow myself to be remarkable

Life is remarkable

I have mastered the virtue remarkable

I know how to live my daily life with remarkability

I know how to live my daily life being remarkable

I have Creator's definition of remarkable

My definition of remarkable is the same as Creator's

I see the remarkableness in every person

My life is remarkable

I am remarkable

I see the world with remarkable clarity

My life is filled with remarkability

I am comfortable being remarkable

I live a remarkable life

I am safe living a remarkable life

I appreciate remarkableness

I am grateful for remarkableness

I know Creator's perspective on remarkable and mine is the same

I am comfortable with remarkable people

I am worthy of being remarkable

Respectful

Treating all with dignity and courtesy

I am a respectful person

I have Creator's definition of respect

My definition of respect is the same as Creators

I believe in respect

I have a lot of respectful people in my life

I know what it feels like to be respectful

I know what it feels like to have the respect of people

I deserve respect

I have mastered the virtue of respectful

I know how to live my daily life with respectability

I know how to live my daily life being respectful

I radiate respect

I draw respectable people into my life

I have respect

I am respected

It is safe to be respected

I am comfortable being respected

I am respectful of people's feelings

I respect myself

I am allowed to respect myself

I am well respected

The next download allows you to insert a name or title

I am respected by _____(add a name or title)

I live my life with respect for people

I am grateful for respect

I appreciate respect

I know when to be and how to be respectful

I am safe being respectful

I am gracious when I show respect

I show respect with humility and kindness

Responsible

Willingness to be accountable for what is ours to do

I am a responsible person

I have Creator's definition of responsibility

My definition of responsibility is the same as Creators

I know what it feels like to be responsible

I know how to live my daily life with responsibility

I know how to live my daily life being responsible

I see the world filled with responsible people

I draw responsible people into my life

I believe in being responsible

I have mastered the virtue responsible

I know how to be responsible

I am comfortable being responsible

I understand how to be responsible

My life is filled with responsible people

I radiate responsibility

Resilient

Recovers from adversity with faith and endurance

I am resilient

I am a resilient person

I have Creator's definition of resilient

My definition of resilient is the same as Creators

I allow myself to be resilient

I have mastered the virtue resilient

I know how to live my daily life with resiliency

I know how to live my daily life being resilient

I believe in resiliency

I allow myself to be resilient

I know resilient people

I see the world as resilient

I radiate resiliency

I appreciate resilient people

I respect resiliency in people

I am comfortable around resilient people

Restraint

Holding back emotions or actions

I have Creator's definition of restraint

My definition of restraint is the same as Creators

I am comfortable with restraint

I have mastered the virtue restraint

I know how to live my daily life with restraint when necessary

I know when and how to use restraint

I know how lovingly exercise restraint

People exercise restraint with me

I know how to hold my tongue

I know how to remain silent

I know when to remain silent

I know it is possible to be silent

I know how to use restraint with my words

I know how to use restraint with my actions

I have mastered the virtue restraint

Righteous

Impeccable integrity that stays on track

I am righteous

I have Creator's definition of righteousness & Righteous

My definition of righteousness and righteous is the same as Creators

I believe in righteousness

I know how to live my daily life with righteousness

I know how to live my daily life being righteous

I know how to be righteous

I have mastered the virtue righteous

I draw righteous people into my life

I have righteous people in my life

I believe in living a righteous life

I see the world filled with righteous people

I know what it feels like to be righteous

I know what it feels like to have righteousness

I radiate righteousness

≫Sensitivity≪

Awareness of vibrations or empathetic to emotions

I am sensitive

I know what sensitivity feels like

I am allowed to be sensitive

I radiate sensitivity

I have mastered the virtue sensitivity

I know when to exercise my sensitivity

It is safe for me to be sensitive

I am allowed to be sensitive

I understand the sensitivity of people

I use my sensitivity in the best of ways

I am energetically sensitive to _____ (add word or choice)

I am sensitive to the feelings of all people

I am sensitive to the feelings of _____ (add name or title)

I am tuned into the sensitivities of people

I use my sensitivity skills for the betterment of all

I am free from being overly sensitive

Serenity

Tranquil trust that all will be well

I believe in Serenity

I have Creator's definition of serenity

My definition of serenity is the same as Creators

I am surrounded by serene people

I expect people to be serene

I know how to live my daily life with serenity

I know how to live my daily life being serene

I am allowed to be serene

I am a master of the virtue serenity

I know serenity

I live my life in serenity

I see the world full of serene people

My life is serene

I love serenity

I know what it feels like to be serene

I know what it feels like to have serenity

I radiate serenity

❧Service❦

Doing helpful things that make a difference

I know how to be of service to people

I have Creator's definition of service

My definition of service is the same as Creators

I am allowed to be of service

I allow myself to be of service

I am a service to others type of person

I am safe being of service to others

I know how to live my daily life with service

I know how to live my daily life being of service

I am comfortable being of service to others

I love being of service

I believe in service

I know how to be of service to humanity

I know how to be of service to all life forms on earth

I know how to be of service to all species

I know what it feels like to be of service to all species

I know what it feels like to be of service when I choose to

I know how to be of service when I choose to

It is safe for me to be of service when I choose to

I enjoy being a service to others type of person

I am comfortable being a service-to-others person

I respect service-to-others type of people

I respect people who live in service

I am grateful for people's service

I am always thankful for good service

Significant

Important and worthy of attention

I am significant

I have Creator's definition of significant

My definition of significant is the same as Creator's

I know what being significant feels like

I am a significant person

I know how to live my daily life with significance

I know how to live my daily life being significant

I know how to be a significant person

I know how to teach people to be significant

I know all people are significant

I know what it feels like to be significant

I know what it feels like to have a significant other

I know I am allowed to have a significant other

I know how to draw a significant other into my life

I am comfortable being significant

I radiate significance

≈Sincere≈

A truthful heart that is genuine

I am sincere

I have Creator's definition of sincere

My definition of sincere is the same as Creators

I am allowed to be sincere

It is safe for me to be sincere

I am a master of the virtue sincerity

I know how to live my daily life with sincerity

I know how to live my daily life being sincere

I know what it feels like to be sincere

I expect people to be sincere

I allow people to be sincere to me

I am comfortable with sincerity

I am a sincere person

I believe in sincerity

I radiate sincerity

᭬Sobriety᭬

Serious claim. Free from intoxication

I have Creator's definition of sobriety

My definition of sobriety is the same as Creators

I am comfortable with sobriety

I am comfortable being sober

I am worthy of being sober

I know what it feels like to be sober

It is safe for me to be sober

I know how to live my daily life with sobriety

I know how to live my daily life being sober

I know I am allowed to be sober

I am strong in my sobriety

I am sober for years

I have mastered the virtue sobriety

My sobriety is important to me

I am allowed to be sober

I allow myself to be sober

I know how to follow the steps of sobriety

I am successful following the steps of sobriety

I know what it feels like to be sober all the time

I am safe being sober

I radiate sobriety

I am worthy of sobriety

I respect the sobriety of people

I understand what sobriety means

I am at peace with sobriety

I am comfortable around friends who are not sober

I stand strong in my sobriety

I can go to a party and be comfortable with sobriety

❧Spiritual☙

Concern with things of the soul, reverence or Higher Power

I am a spiritual person

I know what it feels like to be a spiritual person

I know Creator's definition of spiritual and spirituality

My definition of spiritual and spirituality is the same as Creator's

I know what it feels like to be a spiritual person

I am spiritually evolving in this lifetime

I am safe learning about spirituality

I am evolving spiritually in this lifetime

I know how to live my daily life with spiritual alignment to Creator

I know how to live my daily life being spiritually aligned with Creator

Spiritual people surround me

I am a master of the virtue spiritual

I draw spiritual people into my life

I see humanities spirituality growing in the highest and best of ways

My chakras are spiritually aligned

I allow myself to be a spiritual person

I am a spiritual person

I radiate spirituality

I am allowed to be spiritual

I believe in evolving spiritually

My heart an mind are tuned to my spiritual development

Humanity is evolving spiritually

We all have a right to evolve spiritually

I believe the collective consciousness on earth is evolving spiritually

Spiritual teachers come to me when I am ready

I am mindful of my spirituality

I expect a spiritual mate in my life

I am a spiritual person living a human experience

❧Tactful❧

Deep awareness of speaking kind words of truth

I am a tactful person

I have Creator's definition of tact, tactfully & tactful

My definition of tact, tactfully & tactful is the same as Creators

I expect people to be tactful

I know what it feels like to be treated tactfully

I know how to live my daily life with tactfulness

I know how to live my daily life being tactful

I am always tactful

I know how and when to be tactful

I am allowed to be tactful

I have mastered the virtue tactfulness

It is safe for me to be tactful

I allow myself to be tactful

I believe in being tactful

I know how to treat people tactfully

᷅Tenacious᷄

Good at remembering or stubbornly unyielding

I have Creator's definition of tenacity and tenacious

My definition of tenacity and tenacious is the same as Creators

I am comfortable with tenacity

I know how to live my daily life with tenacity

I know how to live my daily life being tenacious

I am comfortable being tenacious

I have mastered the virtue tenacious

I am worthy of tenacity

I know what it feels like to be tenacious

I am tenacious

I know when and how to be tenacious

I am comfortable around tenacious people

I am safe being tenacious

I respect tenacity in people

I am grateful for tenacious people

Thankful

An attitude of gratitude

I am a thankful person

I have Creator's definition of thankful and thankfulness

My definition of thankful and thankfulness is the same as Creators

I know what it feels like to be thankful

I have mastered the virtue thankfulness

I know how to live my daily life with thankfulness

I know how to live my daily life being thankful

I expect people to be thankful

I know how and when to be thankful

It is safe for me to be thankful

I am allowed to be thankful

J allow myself to be thankful

I believe in being thankful

I appreciate thankfulness

I am always thankful for my life

I am thankful for the path I am living

❧Thoughtful❦

Kindnesses that brighten people's lives

I am a thoughtful person

I have Creator's definition of thoughtful and Thoughtfulness

My definition of Thoughtfulness is the same as Creator's

I know what it feels like to be thoughtful

I know how to live my daily life with thoughtfulness

I know how to live my daily life being thoughtful

I know how and when to be thoughtful

It is safe for me to be thoughtful

I radiate thoughtfulness

I expect thoughtfulness from people

I know what it feels like to be treated thoughtfully

I know what it feels like to receive thoughtfulness from people

I am thoughtful of people's differences

The next download allows you to insert a name or title

I am thoughtful of _____ (add names or titles)

I am allowed to be thoughtful

I allow myself to be thoughtful

I believe in being thoughtful

I am comfortable around thoughtful people

I appreciate thoughtfulness

I am grateful for thoughtful people

I know when to be thoughtful to people

I teach people how to be thoughtful

Thoughtful teachers come into my life

I respect thoughtfulness

I remember when to be thoughtful

I look for opportunities to be thoughtful

I know how to accept thoughtfulness from people who give it to me

I am worthy of thoughtfulness from people

I graciously accept thoughtfulness from people

Tolerant

Acceptance with grace and humor coupled with patience with differences

The next download allows you to insert a name or title

I am tolerant of _____(add name or title of your choice)

I have Creator's definition of tolerance, tolerance and tolerant

My definition of tolerance, tolerant and tolerate is the same as Creator's

I am a tolerant person

I radiate tolerance

I exercise tolerance when upset with people

I know what it feels like to exercise tolerance

I know how to tolerate people

I am a master of the virtue tolerance

I know what it feels like to tolerate people

I know I am tolerant

It is safe for me to be tolerant

I know how to live my daily life with tolerance

I know how to live my daily life being tolerant

It is safe for me to exercise tolerance

It is safe for me to tolerate people

I am filled with grace when I tolerate people

I know the difference between tolerance and judging

I exercise tolerance towards people with different beliefs

I know what it feels like to be treated with tolerance

I know what it feels like to be tolerated

I know what it feels like for people to be tolerant to me

I know tolerance

I allow myself to be tolerant

I am allowed to be tolerant

I expect people to be tolerant

I believe in being tolerant

I am comfortable with tolerant people

I respect tolerant people

I expect tolerance

I am grateful for people who show tolerance

I always give loving tolerance to people

❧Tranquility❧

Serenely peaceful, quite or undisturbed

I have Creator's definition of tranquility

My definition of tranquility is the same as Creators

I am comfortable with tranquility

I radiate tranquility

I am a master of tranquility

It is safe for me to be tranquil

I know how to live my daily life with tranquility

I know how to live my daily life being tranquil

I am comfortable being tranquil

I am worthy of tranquility

I know what it feels like to have tranquility

I draw tranquil people into my life

Tranquil people surround me

I know when and how to be tranquil

❧Truthful❧

Commitment to honesty and authentic living

I know what it feels like to be truthful

I am truthful

I have Creator's definitions of the variations of truth

My definitions of the variations of truth are the same as Creators

I am truth

I know my truth

I am a master of truthfulness

I can smell the truth

I know the truth when I hear it

I understand how important truth is

My words are truthful

I know how to live my daily life with truthfulness

I know how to live my daily life being truthful

I can feel the truth

I draw truthful people into my life

I trust in truth

I am intuitive about my truth

I know that each person has their own truth because of their life experiences

I am allowed to understand the truth of all people

Truth is my guiding light

Humanity is allowed to know the truth

It's time for all humanity to know the truth

We are allowed to know the truth

It's safe for us to know the truth

It's safe for me to know the truth

I know the truth

I knew what it feels like to know the truth

I am free from fear of knowing the truth

I no longer fear the truth

The truth sets me free

The truth sets humanity free

I am free in the truth

The truth makes positive things happen

I face the truth willingly

I released the fear of knowing the truth

I willingly accept the truth

My reality is based on truth

I am truthful in all things

I am allowed to be truthful

I allow myself to be truthful

I release all no truth from my energetic field

I create my truth

I am allowed to create my truth

It's safe for me to create my truth

I know the truth at the cellular level

I know the truth beyond my cells

I know universal truth

I know the wisdom of universal truth

I am a finder of truth

I speak the truth

I am always truthful

I expect people to be truthful

I believe I am truthful

I am comfortable with the truth

I know what trust and truthful feel like

I know how to be truthful in all situations

Words of truth flow to me when I need to be courageous

&Trustworthy&

Worthy of ones trust by faithfully keeping agreements

I am trustworthy

I have Creator's definition of trustworthy, trusted and trust

My definition of trustworthy, trusted and trust is the same as Creators

I deserve to be treated as trustworthy

I am treated as trustworthy

I allow myself to be trustworthy

I know what it feels like to be trustworthy

I know what it feels like to be treated with trust by people

I am allowed to be trustworthy

I radiate trustworthiness

I radiate trust

I draw trustworthy people into my life

It is safe for me to be trustworthy

I expect people to be trustworthy

I expect people to trust me

It is safe for me to feel trust

I trust

I allow myself to trust people

I know how to live my daily life with trust

I know how to live my daily life being trustworthy

I allow myself to be trusted

I know how to trust and when to trust

I trust myself

I trust my ability as a _____(add title)

I trust my ability to see what I need to see

I trust my ability to understand what I want to know

I trust me

I believe I am trustworthy

I am a teacher who creates trust

My words flow from a position of trustworthiness

I know who to trust completely

I know when to trust completely

I am comfortable around trustworthy people

I am grateful for trustworthiness

I teach people how to trust

I can trust people

❧Understanding❦

Listening and perceiving with accuracy, compassion and insight

I understand we are all different

I have Creator's definition of understanding

My definition of understanding is the same as Creators

I understand we are all unique

I understand we each see the world from our own perspective

I understand the perspective of people

I understand the perspective of _____

I understand what it feels like to be understood

I am understood

I am a master of understanding

I draw understanding people into my life

It is safe for me to be understood

I know how to be understood

I know what it feels like to be understood

I know when to be understood

I understand people

230

I understand the thinking people

I understand how different we all are

I understand we all need to understand

It is safe for me to understand

It is possible for me to understand

I deserve to understand

Humanity deserves to understand

We all deserve to understand

I am understanding

I understand_____ (insert name, situation, titles, things)

Understanding is knowledge

Understanding brings wisdom

I except understanding

I understand

My understanding of_____ grow stronger every day

I am allowed to understand_____ (phrases, things, names, situations…)

I am allowed to understand the truth about myself

I completely understand

I am known to be an understanding person

I am an understanding person

I have the ability to completely understand what I focus on

I know what it feels like to understand

I know what it feels like to understand _____ (add word)

It is safe for me to completely understand

I know how to live my daily life with understanding

I grow more understanding each day

I understand knowledge once kept from me

I understand new knowledge

I understand complex knowledge

I understand how to be wise

I understand how to use my wisdom in the highest of ways

I understand I am wise beyond my years

I understand how to use my full brain and heart

I understand how to _____ (add action)

The next download allows you to insert a name or title

I know how to understand _____ (add name or title)

I expect people to be understanding

Unity

Seeking peace and finding common ground in our diversity

I live in unity

I see the world united in peace

I see a unified world

I radiate unity

I am a master of the virtue unity

I know what it feels like to life in unity with life

I am in unity with all of humanity

I am in unity with all life forms

I know how to live my daily life with unity

I know what it is like to live in unity

I know how to live in unity

I have Creator's definition of Unity, unison and unified

My definition of unity, unified and in unison is the same as Creator's

I understand what unity feels like

I know what it feels like to be in in unison with Creator

I understand unity on all levels

I am united with Source Energy

I know what it feels like to be in unison with Creator

I believe in unity

I am comfortable around unified people

I can be in unity with all people and free from taking on their stuff

I am aligned and in unity with Creator

My thinking is in unity with Creator

My spirit is in unison with Creator

I am grateful for unity

I am grateful for unite people

I am grateful and see a united earth

I look forward to a unified world

I appreciate unity

I respect people who are unified

I see Creator in unity

The next download allows you to insert a name or title

I am safe living in unity with _____(insert name or title)

Unity in marriage is safe with_____

᰾Valiant᰾

Showing courage and dedication

I am valiant

I have Creator's definition of valiant

My definition of valiant and Creator's is the same

I am a valiant leader

I am a valiant _____ (add title)

I radiate valor

I am a master of the virtue valiant

I know how to live my daily life with valor

I draw valiant people into my life

I believe in valor

I am comfortable around valiant people

I expect people to be valiant

I am valor

I respect valiant people

I am grateful for valiant people

I know valiant people

❧Vibrant❦

Full of energy and enthusiasm

I am vibrant

I know what it feels like to be vibrant

I have Creator's definition of vibrant and vibrancy

My definition of vibrant and vibrancy is the same as Creator's

I allow the vibrancy of the Universe to shine within me

I have a vibrant light that shines within

I shine with Creator's vibrant light

I know how to shine vibrantly

I draw vibrant people into my life

I radiate vibrancy

I am a master of the virtue vibrant

I know how to live my daily life with vibrancy

I shine vibrantly from within

I know how to be a vibrant person

I am a vibrant person

I am a vibrant leader

I am a vibrant _____(add title)

I believe I am vibrant

I am comfortable around vibrant people

I appreciate vibrant people

I am grateful for vibrant people

I am comfortable around vibrant people

I allow space in my life for vibrant people

I know Creator's perspective on vibrant people and mine is the same

I live my life with vibrancy

Vitality

Exuberance in physical, mental or emotional strength

I have Creator's definition of vitality

My definition of vitality is the same as Creators

I am comfortable with vitality

I know how to live my daily life with vitality

I draw people with vitality into my life

I radiate vitality

I am a master of the virtue vitality

I am a _____ (add title) filled with vitality

I am comfortable being filled with vitality

I am worthy of vitality

I know what it feels like to be filled with vitality

I respect the vitality of people

I am grateful for my vitality

I understand vitality

I enjoy living life with vitality

❧Vivacious❧

Exhibiting liveliness and high spiritedness

I have Creator's definition of vivaciousness

My definition of vivaciousness is the same as Creators

I am comfortable with vivaciousness

I am comfortable being vivacious

I am a master of the virtue vivacious

I know how to live my daily life with vivaciousness

I accept vivaciousness into my life

I draw vivacious people into my life

I am worthy of vivaciousness

I am a vivacious leader

I am a vivacious _____ (add title)

I am comfortable around vivacious people

I know what it feels like to be vivacious

I radiate vivaciousness

I am vivacious

Wisdom

Accumulated scientific or philosophic knowledge

I am full of wisdom

I know when to use my wisdom

I am wise beyond my years

I radiate wisdom

I am a master of the virtue wisdom

I draw wise people into my life

I have Creator's definition of wisdom & wise

My definition of wisdom & wise is the same as Creators

It is safe for me to use my wisdom

I know how to live my daily life with wisdom

It is safe for me to be wise

I know how to be wise

I am a wise leader

I am comfortable being wise

I am a wise _____ (add title)

I am comfortable using my wisdom

I know how to accept the wisdom of people

I accept the wisdom of people

I accept the wisdom of _____ (add name or title)

I believe I am wise

It is safe for me to be wise

I am comfortable around wise people

I teach people how to be wise

I accept the knowledge that makes me wise

Teachers come to me that show me wisdom

When I am ready wise teachers come to me

I appreciate wisdom

I am grateful for wisdom

I respect wisdom in people

I know that knowledge brings wisdom

I have common sense and know when to share my wisdom

Books come into my life that bring me wisdom

As a teacher I share my wisdom

I want my students to become wise

❧Worthy❧

Quality that merits recognition in a specified way

I am worthy of greatness

I have Creator's definition of worthy

My definition is the same as Creator's

I know what it feels like to be worthy

I know that all are worthy

I am a master of the virtue worthy

I feel the worthiness of all people

I see the worthiness of all people

I know how to live my daily life with worthiness

I radiate worthiness

I know that I am worthy

I know how to behave with worthiness

I am worthy of love

I am worthy of _____ (add choice words)

My worthiness is undeniable

I believe I am worthy

I draw worthy people into my life

I accept the worthiness of people

I accept the worthiness of _____ (add name or title)

I know all people are worthy

All people are worthy

I am a worthy leader

I am a worthy follower

I am a worthy _____ (add title)

Everyone is worthy

I live a worthy life

I am a worthy person

I see worthiness in all people

I expect people to know they are worthy

I teach people to see their worthiness

I see worthiness in all people

I see worthiness in all species

I feel worthy

I feel like I have rediscovered my worthiness

I am grateful for worthiness

I deserve worthiness because I am worthy

I am worthy of love

❧Wonderful❧

Open to the mysteries and beauties of life.

I am a wonderful person

I have Creator's definition of wonderful & wonder

My definition of wonderful an wonder is the same as Creator's

I know the wonders of life

I know how to be wonderful

It is safe for me to be wonderful

I am allowed to be wonderful

I see the world as a beautiful place

I see wonder in all things

I am a master of the virtue wonderful

I know how to live my daily life being wonderful

I see the wonders of the world

I see the wonders of me

I know how to be a wondrous person

I see the wonder in all people

I see how wonderful life is

I know I am wonderful and free from ego

I am allowed to think of myself as wonderful

I allow myself to think that I am wonderful

I appreciate the wonders of the world

I am grateful for the wonders of the world

I see the world through the wonderment of a child

I am comfortable travelling to see the wonders of the world

Life is wonderful

I allow myself to see the wonders of life

I know Creator's perspective on wonderful and mine is the same

I surround myself with wonderful people

I am comfortable around wonderful people

❧Xenoglossy❧

Ability to speak a language that you have never learnt

I know how to be positive xenoglossy

It is safe to be an xenoglossy

I know exactly what I am saying as an xenoglossy

I have Creator's definition of xenoglossy

My definition of xenoglossy is the same as Creator's

I am a fluent in a multitude of languages

I can communicate with people of a variety of languages

I am a master of the virtue xenoglossy

I know how to learn with ease

I am familiar with many languages

I know how to live my daily life with xenoglossy if I choose

I am allowed to know many languages

I am comfortable with xenoglossy

I am comfortable around people with the skill of xenoglossy

I am safe around people who xenoglossy

I allow myself to be xenoglossy

I am allowed to be xenoglossy

I know how to understand what I say

I know how to teach people what I say

I understand people when they speak

I am connected to ancient languages

I am connected to the languages of the universe

I am connected to the universal language of Source

I know how to feel the energy of xenoglossy

Youthful

Feeling, acting or looking young. Able to accept new ideas and trends

I am youthful

I know how to be youthful

I know what youthfulness feels like

I am a master of the virtue youthful

I know how to live my daily life feeling youthful

I have Creator's definition of youthfulness and youthful

My definition of youthfulness and youthful is the same as Creator's

I know what it feels like to be youthful

I know how to respond youthfully

I draw youthful people into my life

I am allowed to be youthful at any age

It is safe for me to be youthful at any age

I am in touch with my youthful side

I radiate youthfulness

I know how to behave youthfully

I am a youthful person

I accept youthfulness in my life

I know how to feel youthful

I appreciate youthfulness

My skin radiates youthfulness

I have a youthful appearance

I surprise people when I tell them my age

My skin is supple and firm

I have a youthful outlook on life

I look youthful

I am comfortable around youthful people

I know Creator's perspective on youthfulness an mine is the same

I am grateful for youthful people

I am grateful for my youthfulness

◈Zealous◈

Having or exhibiting strong passion or enthusiasm for life and faith

I am zealous

I know how to live zealously

I am a zealous person

I know how to live my daily life with zeal

I have mastered the virtue of zeal

I know Creator's definition of zealous and zeal

My definition of zealous and zeal is the same as Creator's

I am a zealous _____ (include a word of choice)

I know how and when to be zealous

It is safe for me to be zealous about what I love

I am zealous in completely positive ways

I am zealous and free from causing harm

I know how to be zealous

I have zeal

❧Finalizing Downloads❦

When I read a list of download I finish them off with the
following,

Would you like to know on all levels past present and future that
you know how to when to where to; that it is safe and possible for
you to; that you can have all these things in the highest and best of
ways and live your daily life with them now?

Say Yes!

May Creator Bless You and Keep You Well Now and Forever.

I hope you benefit greatly from this book of downloads. Keep your
eyes open for additional books on a variety of topics and downloads
in the future

❧About The Author❧

Robin is a Master and Certificate of Science Theta Healing® Practitioner and was an instructor. She has a general diploma in Homeopathy from the British Institute of Homeopathy; is a Level 2 Bach Flower Practitioner; an Essential Oils Practitioner; a Reiki Master and has a Certificate of Herbal Studies from the American College of Healthcare Sciences. She is also trained in locating geopathic stress zones. Her college degrees are an MBA in Healthcare Administration and a second MBA in Marketing Management with a bachelors degree in Behavioral Science. She has been involved in healing modalities for decades.

On a more personal note, Robin is a nature photographer. She also enjoys working with stained glass and collects rocks and minerals.

As a teacher Robin taught Lifespan Development, Childhood Development and Art History 1 & 2 both online and in a classroom for a community college. She has also taught numerous Theta Healing® courses from 3 days to 15 days in length and a few courses on essential oils and spiritual development.

Robin started an online school called COATI+ U. If you would like to know more visit her website at www.coatiplusu.com .

Enjoy Life!

Made in the USA
Middletown, DE
07 June 2020

96958262R00146